access to history

TORIES, UNIONISTS *and* CONSERVATIVES 1815–1914

Second Edition

Duncan Watts

Acknowledgements

The front cover illustration shows *Benjamin Disraeli 1st Earl of Beaconsfield* by Henry Weigall, painted in 1880, reproduced courtesy of Bridgman Art Library.

The publishers would like to thank the following individuals, institutions and companies for permission to reproduce copyright illustrations in this book: British Library, page 134; Mary Evans Picture Library, page 91; Punch, pages 80, 118 and 144.

The publishers would also like to thank the following for permission to reproduce material in this book: Cambridge University Press for the extract from *Lord Liverpool and Liberal Toryism* by W. Brock, Cambridge University Press, 1941; Faber and Faber for the extracts from 'Burnt Norton' by T.S. Eliot, published in *Collected Poems 1909-1962* by T.S. Eliot, Faber and Faber, 1974 and from *Modern British Politics* by Smuel Beer, Faber and Faber, 1969; the table adapted from *The Conservative Party: Peel to Churchill* by Robert Blake, published by Eyre & Spottiswoode. Reprinted by permission of The Random House Group Ltd.

Every effort has been made to trace and acknowledge ownership of copyright. The publishers will be glad to make suitable arrangements with any copyright holders whom it has not been possible to contact.

Orders: please contact Bookpoint Ltd, 130 Milton Park, Abingdon, Oxon OX14 4SB. Telephone (44) 01235 827720, Fax: (44) 01235 400454. Lines are open from 9.00–6.00, Monday to Saturday, with a 24-hour message answering service. Email address: orders@bookpoint.co.uk

British Library Cataloguing in Publication Data
A catalogue record for this title is available from the British Library

ISBN 0 340 802073

First published 2002
Impression number   10 9 8 7 6 5 4 3 2 1
Year   2007 2006 2005 2004 2003 2002

Copyright © 2002 Duncan Watts

Typeset by Fakenham Photosetting Limited, Fakenham, Norfolk
Printed in Great Britain for Hodder & Stoughton Educational, a division of Hodder Headline Plc, 338 Euston Road, London NW1 3BH by Bath Press Ltd, England.

Contents

Preface

To the general reader

Although the *Access to History* series has been designed with the needs of students studying the subject at higher examination levels very much in mind, it also has a great deal to offer the general reader. The main body of the text (i.e. ignoring the 'Study Guides' at the ends of chapters) forms a readable and yet stimulating survey of a coherent topic as studied by historians. However, each author's aim has not merely been to provide a clear explanation of what happened in the past (to interest and inform): it has also been assumed that most readers wish to be stimulated into thinking further about the topic and to form opinions of their own about the significance of the events that are described and discussed (to be challenged). Thus, although no prior knowledge of the topic is expected on the reader's part, she or he is treated as an intelligent and thinking person throughout. The author tends to share ideas and possibilities with the reader, rather than passing on numbers of so-called 'historical truths'.

To the student reader

Although advantage has been taken of the publication of a second edition to ensure the results of recent research are reflected in the text, the main alteration from the first edition is the inclusion of new features, and the modification of existing ones, aimed at assisting you in your study of the topic at AS level, A level and Higher. Two features are designed to assist you during your first reading of a chapter. The *Points to Consider* section following each chapter title is intended to focus your attention on the main theme(s) of the chapter, and the issues box following most section headings alerts you to the question or questions to be dealt with in the section. The *Working on...* section at the end of each chapter suggests ways of gaining maximum benefit from the chapter.

There are many ways in which the series can be used by students studying History at a higher level. It will, therefore, be worthwhile thinking about your own study strategy before you start your work on this book. Obviously, your strategy will vary depending on the aim you have in mind, and the time for study that is available to you.

If, for example, you want to acquire a general overview of the topic in the shortest possible time, the following approach will probably be the most effective:

1. Read chapter 1. As you do so, keep in mind the issues raised in the *Points to Consider* section.
2. Read the *Points to Consider* section at the beginning of chapter 2 and decide whether it is necessary for you to read this chapter.
3. If it is, read the chapter, stopping at each heading or sub-heading to note

down the main points that have been made. Often, the best way of doing this is to answer the question(s) posed in the Key Issues boxes.
4. Repeat stage 2 (and stage 3 where appropriate) for all the other chapters.

If, however, your aim is to gain a thorough grasp of the topic, taking however much time is necessary to do so, you may benefit from carrying out the same procedure with each chapter, as follows:

1. Try to read the chapter in one sitting. As you do this, bear in mind any advice given in the *Points to Consider* section.
2. Study the flow diagram at the end of the chapter, ensuring that you understand the general 'shape' of what you have just read.
3. Read the *Working on...* section and decide what further work you need to do on the chapter. In particularly important sections of the book, this is likely to involve reading the chapter a second time and stopping at each heading and sub-heading to think about (and probably to write a summary of) what you have just read.
4. Attempt the *Source-based questions* section. It will sometimes be sufficient to think through your answers, but additional understanding will often be gained by forcing yourself to write them down.

When you have finished the main chapters of the book, study the 'Further Reading' section and decide what additional reading (if any) you will do on the topic.

   This book has been designed to help make your studies both enjoyable and successful. If you can think of ways in which this could have been done more effectively, please contact us. In the meantime, we hope that you will gain greatly from your study of History.

Keith Randell

1 Introduction

Political parties in Britain can be traced back to the seventeenth century, although the concept of parties is difficult to apply in eighteenth-century political life. Even as late as the early nineteenth century many people were still unsure about their desirability. In the early 1800s, there were still many politicians and commentators who frowned on any attempt to divide people into two groups and saw party as 'faction', something very unpatriotic and disloyal. Parties were only in their infancy and the party system had not yet been properly established. Indeed, as late as 1864 the philosopher and Radical MP, John Stuart Mill, could write a book about representative government in which parties were not even mentioned! The contrast between British politics today and political life in the early nineteenth century is thus very marked.

Edmund Burke, a key figure in the development of conservative thought, and himself an MP until his death in 1807, provided us with a classic definition of parties. He described a party as 'a body of men united, for promoting by their joint endeavours the national interest, upon some particular principle in which they are all agreed'. In his *Thoughts on the Cause of the Present Discontents* (1770), he offered a defence of party as a regular and useful element in political life. He saw the association of like-minded men as a natural form of political activity. He argued that they could achieve more of their goals by acting together to promote their common interests and ideas, than through independent action. Whereas others saw parties as at best divisive and at worst unpatriotic, he saw them as the means by which men's beliefs could be given clear political expression. In his apologia (written justification) for party he argued that they should be founded on 'great leading general principles in government'. Members would generally be in accord with each other, although he did not want them to blindly follow those in charge when their behaviour conflicted with their own convictions.

Burke was not describing the political scene which then existed, and he was aware that his theories were unacceptable to many contemporaries. He pointed the way forward, but until the nineteenth century there was still a general suspicion of party which was equated in many people's minds with conspiracy and factionalism. For the same reason the idea of an official opposition in the House of Commons did not attract any widespread support.

Burke's definition remains broadly valid today, but modern writers on parties would stress that to be in a position to advance their ideas, parties need to win power. With this in mind, a modern definition of a party might be a body of people who join together and broadly agree upon some general principles, and who seek to implement them by achieving power via periodic elections.

1 The Early History of the Conservative Party to 1815

Attempts have been made to trace the origins of political parties back to the time of King Charles I in the seventeenth century. Those who supported one national established Church rather than a series of diverse religious groups and who backed the king against the Puritans have been seen as early Tories. In the Civil War (1642–9) they rallied to the Royalist cause. Keith Feiling, in the first edition of his *History of the Tory Party*, 1640–1714, published in 1924,[1] referred to 'two twin schools of thought ... decisively opposed to each other on the causes which most divide mankind – on religious truth and political power'. Following the work of Sir Lewis Namier in the 1930s, he subsequently modified his position and was uneasy about his use of the word 'party' in the title of his book, although he continued to claim that there had been 'a continuous tradition and some elementary framework of party and a descent of political ideas'.

Some historians have taken 1678 as their starting-point for the beginning of political parties. In that year there was a proposal to exclude Charles II's younger brother, James, the Duke of York, from the throne because of his avowed Roman Catholicism. Those who supported his succession were accused of showing a sympathy for the Catholic Church and the term 'Tory' was used to describe them. An abusive reference, it referred to the Catholic outlaws who lived in the middle, 'bog', counties of Ireland, hence the literal meaning of Tory as 'bog-trotters'.

In the Glorious revolution of 1688, James abdicated to be replaced by the Protestant William of Orange, from Holland. Both Whigs and Tories favoured the abdication, for they had found the Catholic king impossible to work with. But whereas the Whigs welcomed the subsequent reduction in royal authority and the supremacy of parliament, the Tories were attached to the idea of an hereditary succession to the throne and to the predominance of the Crown.

Some historians would claim that after 1688 there remained a clear distinction between Whigs and Tories. There are difficulties with this interpretation of events and attitudes, but many would argue that throughout the following century a recognisable Tory tradition survived intact.

a) Eighteenth-Century Toryism prior to the French Revolution

In the eighteenth century, there were groups of people who called themselves 'Tories', but the word was used very loosely. There was little indication of the survival of Feiling's 'First Tory Party', and in the second volume of his work he wrote that it had 'vanished as though it had never been'. Sir Robert Walpole, the Whig statesman and effectively the first British Prime Minister, purged Tories who had served in local and central government. Essentially, there was a non-party basis for most parliamentary activity from the supremacy of Walpole (1721–42) to the arrival on the scene of the Younger Pitt in 1783, and 'party' virtually disappeared in the middle of the century.

However, there were writers and pamphleteers who still called themselves 'Tories'. One of these was Jonathan Swift who was most famous as the author of *Gulliver's Travels*. He portrayed Whigs as politicians who sought to reduce the king's power, extend religious toleration, and protect the monied rather than the landed interest in the community. By contrast, he described a Tory as a firm supporter of the national interest. Tories were those men whose attachment was not to a particular ministry but to the patriotic cause: men who would 'do their utmost to save their prince and their country, whoever be at the helm'. Swift was anxious to preserve the constitution as by law established. He regretted that parliament had declined into faction, by which he meant groupings of politicians seeking offices of profit from motives of private ambition, status and personal gain.

Many of Swift's contemporaries looked with distrust on any classification of men into two opposing groups, Whigs and Tories, and felt that such divisions had been damaging to the country in the past. In as much as they existed, the distinctions were historical, family and local ones, rather than the result of conflicts over major issues of policy or principle. To talk of parties is, therefore, potentially misleading, although there were plenty of people who liked to refer to themselves by one or other of the two labels. And they do indicate what Professor Gash has called 'types, temperaments, traditions and connections'. Tories emphasised patriotic values, and support for Church and king.

Dr Johnson, the best-known literary genius of the eighteenth century, was in no doubt about his political leanings for he was of the opinion that 'the first Whig was the Devil'. He characterised a Tory as someone 'with an instinctive reverence for what was established, a respect for government and the Crown, a loyalty towards the Church of England and a prejudice in favour of the landed interest'. By contrast, he thought of Whigs as those inclined to innovation, who championed the popular interest (when it suited them to do so), who were jealous of executive power and distrustful of ecclesiastical authority. He was using stereotypes which convey the feel of contemporary modes of thought, but they offer little indication of how people reacted in particular circumstances. Despite his strong preferences he was able to write in 1781, 'a wise Tory and a wise Whig, I believe, will agree [that] ... a High Tory makes government unintelligible [and] ... a violent Whig makes it impracticable'.

For most politicians the over-riding concern was to achieve office and to remain there. Once in power, they frequently behaved as their predecessors had done rather than in the way they had reacted when in opposition. In such a fluid situation the Elder Pitt, a Whig who disclaimed party connection, was often supported by Tories during the middle years of the century.

Yet for Frank O'Gorman[2] a Tory tradition lingered throughout the period, even if it would be misleading '... to argue that the Tory party in any sense survived as a coherent body'. He identifies the willingness of the bulk of Tory country gentlemen to support the Court as a distinguishing feature, and notes that by the 1770s there was developing a conservative alliance between Crown, the government and the gentry. The issue which brought this about was the struggle of the American colonies for independence from Great Britain, an issue on which these groups supported a policy of coercion to put down the American rebellion. O'Gorman sees this as the beginnings of the 'conservative reaction' which is more usually dated from the French Revolution of 1789.

b) The French Revolution

The pattern of political behaviour was disturbed by the French Revolution which sparked off a fundamental debate about the manner and pace of change in society, and in so doing fractured the alignment of party groups. Opinions cut across traditional ties, and in Britain former friends and partners found themselves at loggerheads. At first, some people welcomed the upheaval in France as a liberation. They saw it as the dawn of liberty in a country long oppressed by Bourbon rule, and hoped that it might lead to the development of a constitutional monarchy. From the beginning, others were suspicious of what was happening.

Burke was originally a prominent Whig, although he has gone down in history as the father of modern Conservative thinking. He was not convinced that the circumstances of such a revolt could yield a beneficial outcome. He wrote his *Reflections on the Revolution in France* in November 1790, after the fall of the Bastille, but before the imprisonment and eventual execution of Louis XVI, the outbreak of war and the Reign of Terror. He had long supported ancient liberties and rights, but he did not see the Revolution as a means of protecting them. He saw no genuine comparison with England in 1688 and believed that others who did not share any commitment to liberty would exploit the apparently liberal beliefs of the early French revolutionaries. The outcome would be at best weakness and anarchy, at worst bloodshed and tyranny. He dismissed the theorists of revolution as naive in their optimism of a better future, and claimed that 'in the groves of their academy, at the end of every vista you can see the gallows'.

He stressed the need for an ordered society 'to liberate the best elements in mankind, and restrain the worst'. Society must develop naturally as an organic entity with its own character and at its own pace. There was an important place for religion and morality. Rulers ought to rule with restraint as they maintained social order, whilst the governed needed to accept certain basic values which made possible a civilised existence. In this way, the social fabric of a country could be preserved.

Despite his reverence for the past, its social structure and institutions, Burke was not a blind reactionary. He regarded some change as necessary. His previous record had shown a dislike of cruelty, and on issues such as slavery, the rights of Catholics and independence for the American colonies there was an enlightened strain in his thinking. He argued that the maintenance of the status quo must never become so rigid that change could not occur, for as he remarked, 'a state without the means of some change is without the means of its conservation'.

Although he recognised that an unwillingness even to contemplate change could provoke just the violent upheaval in society of which he so despaired, he was very uneasy about any democratic stirrings at home and was alarmed by signs of discontent in the industrial areas where radical opinion was becoming more organised. His wish to see the nation rally to fend off such radical subversion was widely shared. Many people of conservative persuasion feared that there was a serious threat to the landed classes in particular, and more generally to the whole existing social order. Burke's writings gave classic expression to their fears. They also liked his emphasis upon the importance of the Church in society, for some of them had noticed an anti-religious drift in France as the Revolution unfolded. For these reasons he became a popular figure among the aristocrats who had shunned him for years. The occasional extravagance of his language had led some to regard him as suspect in his judgement of issues, but on this occasion his views seemed to be vindicated by events. Many people were shocked at the speed with which the Revolution entered an aggressive phase, with violence and cruelty quickly followed by dictatorship.

A section among the Whigs lost any initial enthusiasm for the events of 1789 once the French monarchy fell and the Revolutionaries talked of aiding revolution everywhere. The threat to the hereditary principle and to the rights of property in Britain caused them alarm, and some of them crossed the floor of the Commons in 1794. Hating what he heard from France, Burke went with them and joined the coalition led by William Pitt the Younger in the hope of helping the country to weather the storm, for since 1793 Britain and France had been at war. After leaving the Whigs, Burke became more opposed to political and social change, for he was appalled by the extreme radicalism of the Jacobin faction then ruling

France. In a comment which reflects his new political allegiance, he spoke in 1796 of 'the cackling of us poor Tory geese' as he issued warnings about the need for stronger national defence. By then, a year before his death in 1797, he was suggesting that one-fifth of the British people had pro-Jacobin sympathies.

Burke provided the first explicit analysis of Conservatism and he is often seen as the founding father of the modern creed. His observations are of enduring value and the *Reflections* are a highly influential text for those who wish to delve into right-wing political thinking. Expressed in fine literary style and highly quotable, the work, in Norman Gash's words,[3] 'outlived his age, because it was based not simply on the historical circumstances of his time but on a profound insight into the nature of man in society'.

After Burke and some other Whigs had joined with the supporters of the Younger Pitt, and were accepting office or pledging support in the House of Commons, British political life was characterised by a cautious conservatism in the conduct of affairs. The Whigs shrunk to a solidly Foxite element – named after their leader, Charles James Fox, who had welcomed the Revolution as the dawn of liberty in France.

c) William Pitt

In entering into war with France, Pitt had no ideological end in view, whereas Burke was concerned to extinguish the flame of revolution in order to stop it spreading further afield. Although Pitt later rallied the country using rhetoric which echoed Burke's sentiments and spoke of 'the liquid fire of Jacobinical principles destroying the world', his motives were more practical. In his view, Britain was fighting primarily to defend its commercial and colonial interests.

Pitt became Prime Minister in December 1783. He was 24. At the time he took office, Fox mocked him as a schoolboy head of a 'mince pie administration', doomed to end as soon as the seasonal mince pies were consumed – yet he remained as Premier until 1801. His career was his life. He never married and he devoted all his time and energy to serving the nation. He brought exceptional gifts of character to the task. More of an administrator than a politician, he was intelligent, industrious, pragmatic, patient and determined. In the House of Commons he was a skilful orator in an age of great debaters, and he established a towering ascendancy. He also had a reputation for aloofness and inaccessibility.

When he first became Prime Minister he could not always be sure of securing full backing for his policies. Cabinet members often differed in their opinions. But he was the man whose views mattered, and he established a pre-eminence over his colleagues. He was popular in the country and well regarded in the commercial world. He dominated British political life much as Sir Robert Peel was to do a generation later, and there was no real rival as an acceptable head of the government. Under his leadership the position of Prime Minister developed in significance for he believed that:

> There should be an avowed and real minister possessing the chief weight in council and the principal place in the confidence of the king. In that respect, there can be no rivalry or division of power. That power must rest with the person generally called the First Minister.

Pitt tried to co-ordinate the policy of the government to give it a clear sense of direction, and he accustomed people to the idea of administrative and financial competence. He set an example of personal honour and integrity, and within the public service showed zeal in seeking high standards of behaviour and good value for money. William Huskisson, later himself to be a senior Cabinet Minister in the early nineteenth century, observed that 'everything that drops from him is ... marked by superior virtue and superior sense'. Huskisson and others of the generation were to become protégés of Pitt, but the Prime Minister was never a strong party figure and had only a small band of personal followers.

Pitt had initially felt some sympathy for the moderate French revolutionaries and had hoped that France 'would soon enjoy just that kind of liberty which I venerate'. But he became alarmed as that country lapsed into a cycle of terror and aggression. He hoped to avoid war, but an active French foreign policy meant that the impact of the Revolution was spreading into Europe. Pitt was troubled by the possible threat to British interests and European order, and his anxiety was widely shared. When France declared war on Britain in February 1793, Pitt had the support to make him the obvious war leader. He tried to unite the country in its patriotic endeavour, and had the rhetorical gifts necessary to inspire the nation, if not the tactical grasp of warfare. Inevitably, he was in the position of reacting to events across the Channel, and in doing so he showed himself to be a superior statesman to many of his European contemporaries.

The mood of the House of Commons was generally conservative, but in the country at large there had for some time been indications of a growing political consciousness. Radicals had agitated against bad government, electoral corruption and the excessive influence of the Crown. They felt that reform was necessary in order to restore a sound constitution. Hopes of political reform had been dashed when Pitt himself had tried and failed to carry resolutions for moderate parliamentary reform through the House in 1785.

By the 1790s there were a number of Radical societies. Some were aristocratic in tone and were linked with the Foxite group in the Commons. Others were made up of artisans who wanted wholesale reform of the parliamentary system. When some used the French style of address and the language of the Revolution it created alarm among the governing classes who saw them as condoning the violence in

France. One of the Radical heroes was Tom Paine, who in 1791–2 wrote his book *The Rights of Man*. This was a justification of the French Revolution. He personally disliked mob rule, as did many of his supporters, but they were all denounced as 'Jacobins'. In the 1790s the Pitt government turned to repression to crush the societies and this drove popular agitation underground, although it continued to burst forth from time to time. Paine was prosecuted for seditious libel (writing, especially for publication, something which was likely to undermine the government's authority), and *habeas corpus* (the right of every detained person to be brought before a magistrate) was suspended, amid other measures to stamp out disorder. In 1799–1800, the Combination Acts were passed. They outlawed trade unions, because they were thought to be another source of possible sedition.

In 1802 a temporary peace between Britain and France was signed, but by then Pitt was no longer in power. He had wrestled with the problems of Ireland and wanted a just settlement of issues affecting her. He favoured and brought about the Union of Great Britain and Ireland in 1800 but believed that it needed to be followed by other measures of pacification. In particular, he favoured Catholic Emancipation, the right of Catholics to be able to sit in the House of Commons and to hold public office. Many of his colleagues did not support him this time, and George III was resolute in his opposition. Pitt misjudged the king's reaction and, when he offered his resignation in 1801, it was accepted. He was back in power again between 1804 and 1806. But this was a troubled period and his administration was less successful than his first one had been. He was not to see the end of the war, for he died in 1806, an exhausted man and still only 46 years old. He had come to symbolise the nation's effort and he left behind him a devoted band of admirers who wished to perpetuate his memory.

Chris Patten,[4] a modern Conservative politician and author of *The Tory Case* has detected three strands of thought in the era of Burke, Pitt and the French Revolution – strands which remain an essential part of the party's approach today:

1 First, there was opposition to systems, to political blueprints and to utopianism; this went hand-in-hand with a profound scepticism about the rationalist approach to life. Secondly, there was a defence of property and order, and a belief that society developed organically or natu-
5 rally, in its own way and at its own rate. Thirdly, there was an unashamed patriotism, a defence of Crown and of country, and of the British national interest.

Pitt was not the leader of a well-organised party, with a majority in the House of Commons. He was not the people's choice. He had been chosen by the king, and he stayed in office for as long as he did because he generally enjoyed royal support. He had only a small band of fifty or sixty personal followers, although he and his ministers could usually count on many more who were willing to support anyone who enjoyed Crown backing. Although many writers place Pitt in the Tory tradition, others are uneasy because of one major problem. He was not a Tory, and he never called himself one. He was an independently minded Whig who saw himself as part of a great Whig tradition going back to the Revolution of 1688. Above all, he was not a party politician. He believed that governments should be formed from the best available talent. However, because of his obvious political skills and his approach to public affairs, Conservative writers like to include him in the gallery of their famous predecessors. This is not unreasonable because his attitudes were fundamentally conservative, and his desire for moderate reform accompanied by social discipline among the 'lower orders' at a time of radical unrest, identifies him as a firm supporter of that 'ordered liberty' of which Conservatives frequently speak.

The development of the French Revolution and the growth of radicalism at home helped to polarise opinion between reformer and conservative. On the one hand were those such as Fox who stood for constitutional liberty and progress, and who called themselves Whigs. On the other were those who wished to resist the popular tide and defend the constitution as it was. The second group included landowners and many of the professional and business classes, some of whom were in the process of becoming landowners themselves, as well as the bulk of the clergy. It was reinforced by the 'old Whigs' as Burke sometimes called them, who shared conservative values. It is from this Pittite coalition of forces that something which can be distinguished as Toryism emerged.

d) The Development of Toryism, 1806–11

After Pitt's death a 'Ministry of the Talents' took over. But it did not include the Pittites whose main standard-bearers were George Canning and William Huskisson. They dreamed of one day recreating the old Pitt ministry in the spirit of their dead hero. Meanwhile, they met regularly for political dinners and committed themselves to broad support for the government as long as Pitt's policies were not abandoned. When they detected 'backsliding' they became vigorous in opposition, although with limited success because they lacked leadership and were but one of a number of parliamentary groups. George III replaced the 'Talents' ministry and in the general election which followed soon afterwards, in 1807, those who supported his action, mainly the Pittites, used the label 'Tory' and those who opposed it called themselves 'Whigs'.

Over the next few years the memory of Pitt faded and what held his followers together was no longer just his legacy. It was also a common attachment to upholding the king's policies and position. Spencer

Perceval, Prime Minister between 1809 and 1812, pinpointed this transformation from 'Pittism' to Toryism in his observation that:

> The magic of that [Pitt's] name is in a great degree dissolved, and the principle upon which we must rely to keep us together, and to give us the assistance of floating strength, is the public sentiment of loyalty and attachment to the king.

Following the fall of Pitt's main ministry in 1801 there was a succession of six Prime Ministers in less than 12 years. However, there was considerable continuity in policy for much of the time, and a nucleus of senior ministers was often in office. They stood for the vigorous prosecution of the war against France, discouragement of the radical reform movement at home, an end to discussion of the Catholic question for the time being, and a general responsiveness to the wishes of the monarch.

e) The Beginning of the Liverpool Era

In 1812, after a period of parliamentary confusion, Lord Liverpool took office and formed an administration which was to remain in power for 15 years. Their opponents labelled its members and policies as Tory even if the term was not one that Liverpool would have chosen to employ. It was a Tory ministry because it upheld just the sort of attitudes that Pitt had represented in the 1790s and which had become widely accepted platitudes by 1812 – namely loyalty to Church and king, the maintenance of law and order at home, and defence of the nation's security from external threat. As the Opposition was happy to be thought of as 'Whig' it was natural that the government should be seen as 'Tory' whether or not it approved of the use of the label. Furthermore, although Liverpool still thought of himself as primarily a servant of the king rather than as a party spokesman, unlike Pitt he was willing to organise a parliamentary following for his government.

For Liverpool, Burke was the greatest philosopher and Pitt the greatest statesman who had ever lived. Since the day that Burke crossed the floor and supported the Pittite coalition there has been, in Blake's words,[5] a 'continuous and definable Tory tradition'. As he observed, the attitudes of a person who was a Tory near the beginning of the nineteenth century would have been recognisable to his counterpart today.

2 The Tory/Conservative/Unionist Place in the Two-Party System

In as much as recognisable parties existed at the beginning of our period, they were not separated by a fundamental disagreement over political ideals, nor did they represent very different social backgrounds. They were loosely held together, often as a result of historical and family ties, and differed only in their general approach to matters of policy. By then, there were two main parties, the Tories being the grouping more reluctant to embrace change and the Whigs being a little less fearful of innovation. In 1815 many MPs did not class themselves as belonging to either grouping. They considered themselves to be Independents. However, there were many cliques and factions, which were seen as either generally friendly towards the government or as generally opposed to it. The Tories were only able to remain in office until 1830 by winning the backing of enough of these factions and of these unaligned members to secure a majority in the important votes. In the 1830s the division between the parties became more clear-cut, and the two-party system began to function, with Whigs on the one side, and Tories (or Conservatives, as the party, now under the leadership of Sir Robert Peel, was generally known), on the other. There followed a period of confusion and instability after the Conservative Party broke up over the repeal of the Corn Laws in 1846, but by 1867 the two-party system had reasserted itself. The Whigs had evolved into the Liberal Party and the Tories were universally known as the Conservative Party. Thereafter, Conservative and Liberal administrations succeeded each other, normally without having to think about the need for third-party support, as they were able to form a strong administration with a clear majority in the House of Commons.

In 1882, W.S. Gilbert was able to write the famous lines of his popular comic opera *Iolanthe* which pinpointed the basic divide in English politics:

1 I often think it's comical
   How often nature does contrive
   That every boy and every girl,
   That's born into the world alive,
5 Is either a little Liberal,
   Or else a little Conservative!

In essence he was broadly correct, although, as we shall later see, there were other groups and parties at various times, such as Radicals, Peelites and Liberal Unionists.

On the continent, where the tendency is for there to be more political parties than there are in the United Kingdom, parliamentary assemblies are designed differently to our House of Commons in which two rows of benches facing each other generally suits an essentially two-party system. In the most European countries seating is arranged in a semi-circular chamber. This allows as many parties as there are to be seated coherently and for representatives to sit according to their political affiliation – more conservative ones to the right, more radical ones (who in various degrees favour change) to the left. This has given rise to the terms 'Right' and 'Left' which are commonly used in this country. The party of the Left in nineteenth-century Britain was to be the Liberal Party, and what became the Conservative Party was on the political Right, as it is today.

The title of this book indicates that, although in its essential attitudes the party remained the same, its name changed. The word 'Tory' was, as we have seen, originally an abusive one employed by its opponents. It remained as the party label until 1830–32. 'Conservative' gradually crept in, and by the mid-1830s it was well established. It implied that the party was seeking to broaden its appeal to include all the conservative forces which were opposed to the Whigs. Even after the break-up over the Corn Laws, when Peel's 'new Conservative Party' suffered a devastating setback, the term was still used, although the young Disraeli did something to bring 'Tory' back into fashion. He was keen to place himself in a long Tory tradition which pre-dated Peel's leadership and which placed a greater emphasis upon the preservation of institutions and of the old social order.

By 1886 it was the Liberals' turn to split (over Home Rule for Ireland), and those who broke away, such as the Radical, Joseph Chamberlain, and the Whig, Lord Hartington, saw themselves as 'Liberal Unionists'. They believed in the union of Britain and Ireland, as brought about in 1800, and shared this attitude with Lord Salisbury and the Conservatives. In time, these Liberal Unionists became more closely identified with the Salisbury governments, and some of them served in his final administration, which was a Conservative and Liberal Unionist one. The shorter term 'Unionist' was frequently used by politicians and commentators to describe those who belonged to the conservative cause, although it was not until 1911 that the Liberal Unionists and the Conservatives formally merged, to become the Conservative and Unionist Party of today.

Under whatever label they operated, the Conservatives rested their support primarily upon the landed interest. However, as land lost its overwhelming importance in society with the onward march of industrialism, the party reached out to appeal to and incorporate those who obtained their wealth from other sources, such as the owners of commercial and industrial undertakings.

3 The Nature of Conservatism

Michael Oakeshott[6] has defined Conservatism as 'not a creed or a doctrine, but a disposition'. This disposition leads its adherents to favour what already exists, for 'a known good is not lightly to be surrendered for an unknown better'. In this remark, we see the cautious approach of Conservatives to change. They have an instinctive preference for society as it is: the very name implies a desire to preserve what already exists. In Britain, this has not meant hostility to all change. Merely to wish to defend the status quo or to put the clock back to some bygone age is not Conservatism – it is blind reaction. The point was well made by Peter Viereck:[7]

1 Not all the past is worth keeping. The conservative conserves discriminately, the reactionary indiscriminately. Though the events of the past are often shameful and bloody, its lessons are indispensable. By 'tradition', the conservative means all the lessons of the past, but only the
5 ethically acceptable events. The reactionary means all the events.

The emphasis is upon preserving the best of the past, for as Burke argued, 'a disposition to preserve and an ability to improve, taken together, would be my standard of a statesman'. For Conservatives there is a preference for continuity. They feel that the onus of proof rests on those who wish to make changes.

Conservative ideas are not easy to summarise, for as Ian Gilmour has written[8] 'so far, then, as philosophy or doctrine is concerned, the wise Conservative travels light'. Conservatives distrust ideology and dogma, and do not believe that society can be improved by making changes founded on some belief in human progress and the perfectibility of man. They have a general dislike of all-embracing theories and of preconceived blueprints for action. They distrust plans and detailed programmes and are often said to be 'pragmatic and empirical' in their search for practical solutions to problems; in other words, their ideas are based on observation and practical experience, rather than theory. It is perhaps significant that most of the writing about Conservative thought has been done by practising politicians, such as Burke, Disraeli, Lord Hugh Cecil and Ian Gilmour, rather than by political philosophers.

There is no unchanging body of doctrine in Conservatism. Because Conservatives distrust abstract reasoning, they adjust their policies in the light of experience and circumstances. They are sceptical of any proposal which seems to conflict with human nature, and dislike change for the sake of change. Their approach to change is evolutionary, building upon the foundations of the past whilst adapting to changing conditions. Adaptation has been the key to British Conservatism for, as Disraeli recognised, the Conservatives have never believed in finality. But the adaptation needs to be carried out in the way he described in 1867, 'in deference to the manners, the customs, the laws and the traditions of a people'. Although some Conservatives have been more rigid in their thinking than others, most have accepted the need to adjust as time passes. Lord Salisbury, himself no progressive in the Party, once described the commonest political error as 'sticking to the carcasses of dead policies'. Supporters of the this approach would argue that this shedding of obsolete shibboleths (outworn slogans) has had more to do with realism than with lack of principle, for pragmatism is a key element of Conservative politics.

If it is the case that, in Anthony Seldon's words,[9] the party is one 'of instincts (above all for power) rather than of ideology', there are nonetheless certain elements of continuity in the attitudes to which Conservatives in times past and today subscribe. They include a preference for established institutions, the maintenance and promotion of the national interest and support for private property and free enterprise. Some or all of these ingredients are to be found in the thinking of Burke and other Conservatives who have contributed to the stream of party thinking.

a) Burkeian Themes

Many strands of thinking have contributed to Conservative thought. The party is a reflection of its past and has been described[10] as 'a river into which many tributaries have flowed'. Yet certain ideas have regularly recurred over the years and have been accepted by many Conservatives in every generation – the importance of religion, the desirability of social stability, the rule of law, and the necessity of upholding civil and political liberty. Burke, writing at the time of the French Revolution, expressed many of them.

Burke stressed the importance of religion and the value of its recognition by the state. He saw it as 'the basis of civil society, and the source of all good, and of all comfort'. Many Conservative writers since then have taken the view that men and women, with all their imperfections, can never be made better by legislation. They believe that if those individuals base their behaviour on a religious view of life, then it is more likely that their lives will be enriched and their duties to others fulfilled. In the nineteenth century there was a close link between the Church of England (the Anglican Church) and the Tory Party. The Church was often portrayed as the Tory Party at prayer, and on matters ranging from education to the granting of full civil freedom to Roman Catholics, the maintenance of the supremacy of the Church was seen as important by many supporters.

Burke also disapproved of equality and desired to maintain rank and station. It was fundamental to Tory thinking that society is basically hierarchical, based on class, and requires authoritative leadership in order to maintain stability. The governing class provides the authoritative leadership, because the art of government requires exceptional talent. It can be practised successfully only by a few, who are in consequence entitled to wealth and privileges to distinguish them from the rest of society. The governed will accept those who govern them because of their obvious talent for leadership and because of a feeling of deference (respect) towards the ruling class. In this way the idea of authoritative leadership, which has its origins in the period before the extension of the franchise, could be later reconciled with the democratic tradition which emerged as a result of mass suffrage. According to this view, the role given to the electorate is a limited and passive one. They do not initiate policy, which comes down from their leaders. Conservatives could 'Trust the People' in the confident expectation that the people would respond by choosing them to rule.

Underlying this approach was a defence of the established order in society, a theme caught well in a verse of the Victorian hymn, *All Things Bright and Beautiful*:

The rich man in his castle,
The poor man at his gate.
God made them high and lowly
And ordered their estate.

Tories had no intention of changing this balance in society, although the more paternalistic among them wanted to ensure that those who were 'lowly' could enjoy a decent standard of life.

Burke also strongly supported the institution of private property, and was opposed to any injustice being done to individuals in the course of political and social reform. The desire to avoid injustice was a limiting factor on both parties in the nineteenth century and, as a result, state action was viewed with suspicion. Measures to protect workers had a habit of infringing the rights of factory owners, and this made politicians reluctant to interfere with the workings of *laissez-faire* (leave alone).

Finally, Burke believed that change must be evolutionary and must be carried out in accordance with the nature of the society. He viewed the state as being organic, in that, in his words, it was 'a partnership not only between those who are living, but between those who are living and those who are dead, and those who are to be born'. Most Conservatives, who wish to see a link between the past, the present and the future, would share his feelings for continuity. As the twentieth-century poet, T.S. Eliot put it in his poem, *Burnt Norton*:

Time present and time past
Are both perhaps present in time future
And time future contained in time past.

Conservatives of every generation would echo Burke's dislike of violent change and would wish to see evolution rather than revolution. 'Ordered change' is a phrase much used by Conservative writers.

b) Adaptation in the Nineteenth Century

Much of what Burke wrote was accepted by his successors in the nineteenth century. They usually stressed the need for change to be accomplished in a peaceful, gradual manner which did not infringe the rights of others. Their thinking lacked rigidity, for it was not doctrinaire. Conservative politicians in office were rarely willing to repudiate all innovation. Canning, a progressive Tory of the 1820s, made the point that those who refuse all improvements because they are innovations often find themselves forced to accept innovations when they have ceased to be improvements. In this spirit, Conservative leaders were to give way on a number of occasions. Sometimes changes were made only grudgingly and acceptance was delayed as long as possible. On other occasions Conservatives initiated change. Even in its most negative period (the years before the First World War), the Party did not quite opt to die in the last ditch.

In the 1830s Peel created a tradition of moderate Conservatism. Although he believed in the importance of established institutions, he placed less emphasis upon traditional Tory values than many in the Party would have wished. His fall in 1846 placed the whole movement in jeopardy, and it was his arch-opponent over the Repeal of the Corn Laws, Disraeli, who made the larger input to Tory thinking. He desired to uphold cherished institutions such as the Monarchy and the Church. He also thought in terms of a natural alliance between the aristocracy and the people, and espoused popular principles:

> The Tory party is only in its proper position when it represents popular principles. Then it is truly irresistible. Then it can uphold the throne and the majesty of the empire, the liberty of the nation, and the rights of the multitude.

Many of his ideas have had an influence on the modern party. His Tory Democracy may have been a vague and romantic notion rather than a concrete reality, but he taught the Conservative Party that policies serving only the interests of one class could only be justified if they were genuinely designed to serve the national good rather than a sectional interest. He laid claim to a Conservatism which transcended class barriers and was representative of the needs and aspirations of the whole community. It was patriotic abroad and similarly stressed national interests at home.

c) Differing Conceptions of Conservatism

Throughout their histories the Tory and Conservative Parties, like most others, have been coalitions made up of people with significantly differing views. The Tory tradition dates back to the time when the landed interests dominated public life and, at their best, exhibited a decent paternalism in the conduct of affairs. Its members were, on occasion, prepared to use state power to improve living conditions. As the nineteenth century progressed and business interests became more important in the Conservative Party, the commercial and industrial values of the middle classes assumed greater significance. Its representatives stressed the freedom of businessmen to further their own interests, and shared the *laissez-faire* approach of many Liberals. They believed that it was not the government's role to regulate economic and social life and were suspicious of state intervention. The Liberal Unionist input of Whigs and the Chamberlainites emphasised these beliefs, stressing the importance of the individual and of individual enterprise. Modern Conservatism still contains exponents of both approaches, Tories and *laissez-faire* liberals, though neither line of argument is normally allowed to dominate party thinking completely.

Donald Southgate[11] has distinguished three viewpoints common to the Conservative approach and has found a quotation from Lord Salisbury to illustrate each one. The 'Diehard view' was expressed in a comment made in 1859: 'Hostility to radicalism, incessant, implacable hostility, is the essential definition of Conservatism'. He sounded a little less uncompromising in 1863, when he spoke of '[contenting] ourselves with patching a little here, and altering a bit there'. Such a view, Southgate remarks, was couched 'in rigidly defensive terms, but scope is allowed for flexibility and reform'. Shortly before he first became Prime Minister, he sounded more constructive:

> The object of our party is not and ought not to be simply to keep things as they are. In the first place, the enterprise is impossible. In the next place, there is much in our present mode of thought and action, which it is highly undesirable to conserve.

In this comment he placed himself much more in the lineage of Peel and Disraeli, and was a spokesman for the moderate Conservatism to which many party members would still lay claim.

In their attitude to public affairs people tend to fall into two very broad groups: those who are progressive and anxious to promote change and social improvement, and those who emphasise a desire for continuity and are more conservative in their outlook. Those in the second category prefer to let change come about gradually and this instinct for caution in the conduct of business has always been a strong one. Yet, although there has always been a distinctively conservative approach, there was no organised political party to advance such a viewpoint until the nineteenth century. Then, the division into those who promoted and those who were wary of change became the basis of political loyalties.

References

1 K. Feiling, *History of the Tory Party, 1640–1714* (Macmillan, 1924)
2 F. O'Gorman, *The Emergence of the British Two-Party System 1760–1832* (Arnold, 1990)
3 N. Gash in Lord Butler (ed.), *The Conservatives: a History from their Origins to 1965* (Allen and Unwin, 1977)
4 C. Patten, *The Tory Case* (Longman, 1983)
5 R. Blake, *The Conservative Party from Peel to Major* (Heinemann, 1997)
6 M. Oakeshott, *Rationalism in Politics* (Methuen, 1962)
7 P. Viereck, *Conservatism Revisited* (John Lehmann, 1950)

8   I. Gilmour, *Inside Right: A Study of Conservatism* (Hutchinson, 1977)
9   A. Seldon and S. Ball, *Conservative Century: the Conservative Party since 1900* (OUP, 1994)
10 T. Raison, *Why Conservative?* (Penguin, 1964)
11 D. Southgate, *The Conservative Leadership: 1832–1932* (Macmillan, 1974)

The Age of Lord Liverpool and Beyond, 1815–32

2

POINTS TO CONSIDER

Mindful of recent revolutionary upheavals in France, the government after 1815 placed more emphasis on a firm approach to maintaining law and order than on a policy of redressing popular grievances. In the early 1820s, as memories of the French Revolution grew dimmer, new and younger ministers were responsible for constructive change. They realised that accepting cautious innovation did not necessarily undermine their position; opposing it could have far more dangerous consequences. After Lord Liverpool's death, the divisions within the Party between moderate reformers and High Tories on the Right (the Ultras) could not for long be contained.

The most important political figure during this period was Lord Liverpool. Base your thinking around his personality and his policies. Distinguish between the period when his policies are often described as 'repressive' (1815–22) and the years in which his approach is described as more 'liberal' (1822–7). Look for the elements of continuity and change. Consider the state of the party on his departure and how it coped in the years immediately following his retirement and death.

KEY DATES

1815	Peace returned, with the ending of the wars against France. Corn Laws introduced.
1815–20	'Repression', in response to sporadic rioting around country.
1819	'Peterloo massacre'.
1820	Reconstruction of government.
1822–7	More 'liberal' era.
1827	Lord Liverpool retired and shortly after died.
1827–32	Brief ministries of Canning, Goderich and Wellington.

When Lord Liverpool became Prime Minister in 1812 he was not expected to survive in office for very long. In its early months, his government seemed so insecure that it looked as if it would soon collapse. However, he was fortunate that this period coincided with a revival of Britain's fortunes in the wars against the French, for many people were pleased by Wellington's victories and this made them contented with the government's general handling of affairs. After the return of peace in 1815 the country was beset with problems, but having overcome the early difficulties, Liverpool contrived to remain in office until 1827, and his party continued to do so for three years longer.

The Tories were fortunate to be faced by opponents who, for much of the time, were weak, ineffectual and lacking in strong leadership. The breakaway of some Whigs to join the Pittite coalition in 1794 had seriously demoralised their former party, and for many years it was unable to offer sustained opposition. Divisions within the Whigs' ranks made it easier for the Tory government to fend off defeat in the House of Commons because, although many MPs could not be relied on to back Lord Liverpool and his colleagues, they did not wish to see them overthrown and the Whigs installed in their place. The voters, who made up only 2 per cent of the population, agreed, and the elections of 1818 and 1826 confirmed the government's dominant parliamentary position.

1 Personalities

> **KEY ISSUES** What sort of men were included in the Tory cabinet after 1815? What were their priorities?

The government that Lord Liverpool had formed in 1812 and which had triumphed against Napoleon continued in office after 1815. It contained several members of the old Pittite coalition, notably Lords Eldon, Sidmouth and Castlereagh, as well as the Prime Minister himself. They were joined by younger Tories such as Huskisson, Palmerston and Peel. These men were much influenced by what had happened in France since 1789, where a king and queen had been executed, the nobility decimated, and the whole traditional pattern of life shattered.

a) Lord Liverpool and his Cabinet

An examination of Lord Liverpool's Cabinet, its personnel and their approach, provides a useful insight into the nature of early-nineteenth century Toryism. Historians have not usually written sympathetically of the Prime Minister himself, yet he achieved the feat of surviving as Premier for a longer uninterrupted period than any other leader of the party. It has to be admitted that this was partly due to the lack of a credible alternative for much of the time, but it was also a tribute to his own skill and leadership. His ministry both overcame the initial difficulties it confronted and adjusted itself to the improving conditions of the 1820s.

Lord Liverpool had entered the House of Commons in 1790 as Philip Jenkinson and had moved to the House of Lords on his father's death in 1808. He had undergone a long apprenticeship before he reached the top, serving in numerous ministerial offices. He had not been marked out as possessing obvious prime-ministerial potential, and there were others around him of more outstanding ability. He was not intellectually gifted, was not an original thinker, and had a narrow, unimaginative mind. One French observer noted rather unkindly that if he had been present on the day of creation he would have begged God to preserve chaos! His speeches did not inspire and he was wary of change. Disraeli later recognised some of the flaws in his political make-up when he referred to him in his novel, *Coningsby*, as an 'arch-mediocrity'.

Yet this is not the whole picture for he had useful qualities. His amiable character was much praised by those who knew him well and they recognised his fairness, integrity and dependability. His colleagues liked and trusted him and responded to the free hand he gave them. They could count on his common sense, loyalty and support, and he was able to draw the best out of them. He was also an effective chairman of the Cabinet. By his understated manner he was able to reconcile ministers of widely differing views and maintain harmony. He was not too closely identified with any particular faction and therefore did not antagonise any group. In negotiations he was tactful and he steered a steady and skilful course, making few enemies and winning numerous friends. This emollient (soothing) style of leadership served the government and party well for many years.

Some of the ministers Lord Liverpool appointed were distinctly unimpressive. The Chancellor of the Exchequer, Nicholas Vansittart, lacked any real grasp of his subject. Lord Sidmouth, the Home Secretary between 1812 and 1822, also did not measure up to the demands of the position. Like his colleagues he was unsure how to tackle the post-war unrest, but his attempts to maintain order were clumsy and were widely thought to be unnecessarily repressive. Deeply conservative, he was later to make his last public speech against Catholic Emancipation and to cast his final vote against the 1832 Reform Bill. Lord Eldon, the long-serving Lord Chancellor, helped Sidmouth draw up much of his restrictive legislation, and was a Tory cast in a similar mould. He opposed any modification of the severe criminal code and resisted Catholic Emancipation and other reform proposals. His approach was unyielding and he could not imagine that the constitutional arrangements of the country could be improved.

However, it was Lord Castlereagh who attracted the greatest public odium. This was despite the fact that he was less unbending in his approach and on Irish and economic affairs was relatively forward-looking. In his early days he had even been attracted by some of the ideas of the French revolutionaries. As well as being Foreign Secretary he was Leader of the House of Commons (of which he was allowed to be a member because he was an Irish peer), and he soon gained a reputation as a 'hard-liner'. Because most of his cabinet colleagues were in the House of Lords it was his task to 'sell' the government's unpopular policies in the House of Commons. His awkward and disdainful manner, perhaps born of shyness, made him ill fitted for the task and he often mixed his metaphors and became tongue-tied under pressure. He was viciously lampooned by poets and satirists of the day. It was the poet Shelley who highlighted his cold reserve in the memorable lines of his *Mask of Anarchy*:

1 I met murder on the way
    He had a mask like Castlereagh –
    Very smooth he looked, yet grim;
    Seven bloodhounds followed him:

5 All were fat; and well they might
    Be in admirable plight.
    For one by one, and two by two,
    He tossed them human hearts to chew
    Which from his wide cloak he drew.

Most members of the Cabinet did not belong to the old aristocracy. In several cases their fathers had been professional men or merchants who had made enough money to buy themselves into the landlord class. They were not all hugely rich, but several gave the impression that they were remote and out of touch with the country. Given their backgrounds and outlook, they were easily ruffled by stories of disorder and unrest.

b) Toryism in 1815

The attitudes of the government are often described as traditional 'Church and King Toryism'. Ministers defended the Anglican Church as one of the great institutions of the state and wished to preserve its privileged position as the established church. They tended to be more hostile towards other denominations than were the Whigs. For example, they resisted granting full political rights to both Catholics and non-conformists. They always supported the preservation of royal authority at its current level, even though in 1820 the Prime Minister was to be in sharp disagreement with the new king at the time of the scandal over his private life. They were concerned to preserve order and stability, and in the pursuit of this they laid more emphasis on the rights of property than on the rights of individuals. They stressed the importance of land, rather than of commerce and industry, as the main form of property, and saw the landed interest as an essential bastion of society which they wished to protect at all costs.

Drawing their support from those who wished to maintain the status quo, they opposed political reform and were highly sensitive to any radical protest. The political system served them well, and self-interest made them unwilling to entertain any significant change in it. They did not totally oppose all humanitarian reform, but most members were reluctant to make any concessions at a time when there was evident lawlessness in the country at large. The trouble was that, although they wished to keep things broadly as they were, the country was in a state of transition and upheaval. Many people wanted change and reform.

2 The Situation Around the Country

> **KEY ISSUES** What were the main domestic problems facing the country in the years immediately after 1815? How effectively did members of the Liverpool administration tackle them?

a) Post-war Distress

In 1815 the country was troubled by social and economic difficulties as it moved from war to peace. The fortunes of agriculture and industry were affected by an economic depression in which unemployment and under-employment (short-time working) sharply increased. The situation was worsened by the rapid increase in population and the speedy demobilisation of troops at the end of the war, both of which meant that there were even more people looking for work. This was happening against the background of a country which was changing from a predominantly agricultural to a predominantly industrial one, with urban conditions deteriorating as the expansion of factory towns outpaced the provision of services such as sanitation and piped water. For many people the result was that these were times of hardship and gloom.

Government action aggravated the situation. It passed the Corn Laws in 1815, with Whig support. They were designed to help the agricultural community by banning the import of corn until domestic prices became very high. Those who owned factories and worked in commerce saw this agricultural protection as a likely barrier to their attempts to export goods, for if Britain would not allow in foreign corn foreigners might be unwilling to accept or might not be able to afford our manufactured products. Radicals criticised the laws' likely effects on living standards. It was believed that they would keep the price of corn, and therefore of bread, artificially high. Lord Blake,[1] a historian of Conservative sympathies, has described the laws as 'one of the most naked pieces of class legislation in English history'.

Parliament made another move which benefited its own members and further attacked the living standards of the majority of the population when in 1816 it voted to end the Property (or Income) Tax which Pitt had introduced as a wartime measure. Liverpool and Vansittart saw the continuation of the tax as necessary but they were overruled by the House, which illustrates the difficulty that the government could face in obtaining a Commons majority. To make up the deficiency in government income, ministers had to raise indirect taxes on purchases. This disproportionately hit the less-well-off sections of the community.

Those of radical persuasion believed that members of parliament were looking after their own interests and were unable or unwilling to relieve the suffering around the country. In the hope of changing this situation they campaigned to make the House of Commons more representative of the population as a whole. They saw that the existing, unreformed system with its narrow franchise, rotten and pocket boroughs where at most a few people possessed the right to choose the MPs, and open voting resulted in a chamber in which power was primarily in the hands of the landed interest. They thought that justice would only be done and economic grievances tackled if there was a parliament which reflected all or most sections of the community.

Parliamentary reform became a regular demand in the speeches of radical agitators. However, the discontent around the country between 1815 and 1820 was not based on one issue alone. It arose out of diverse grievances which varied from locality to locality. Bad harvests, high prices for essential goods, unemployment, poor living conditions and the Corn Laws were common complaints which contributed to the growing mood of protest. Whatever the causes, few doubted the widespread extent of the distress and suffering in both agricultural and in industrial areas. Distress provoked feelings of discontent, and at meetings and marches up and down the country the hungry and unemployed gathered to hear radical orators demand reform. Some demonstrations were peaceful, but at others there was considerable violence.

Strikes, marches and petitions often passed off without serious incident, but there were exceptions. In East Anglia, agricultural labourers carried banners inscribed with the message 'Bread and Blood', and rioting was frequent. In industrial towns in the Midlands and North, factory machinery was smashed as a way of making the point that the development of factories was destroying the traditional way of life. Particularly alarming for ministers was the gathering at Spa Fields in December 1816, which got out of control; a mob of demonstrators marched towards the City of London, raiding armourers' shops en route. Such agitation filled the propertied classes with horror, and restrictive measures were almost inevitable.

In 1817, the Home Secretary decided to act. He suspended *Habeas Corpus*, the legal process which prevented any person from being held in prison without trial, and introduced what became known as the Gagging Acts. Among other things, these clamped down on the holding of seditious meetings (meetings championing change in the existing political arrangements). Arrests of prominent agitators, transportation (deportation to a criminal colony) and execution were part of the government's tough response to the widespread agitation, and Sidmouth employed informers and *agents-provocateurs* to find out about future mass protests. These measures – and better harvests – helped to make the rest of the year and 1818 a more tranquil period, but in 1819 tension returned. At St Peter's Field in Manchester anxious magistrates sent the cavalry into the vast, but orderly, crowd which had gathered to hear 'Orator' Hunt, a Radical MP. In the panic which resulted, 11 people were killed and more than 400 were injured. The disaster (popularly known as Peterloo, a parody of Waterloo, the battle at which Napoleon had been defeated four years previously) aroused public indignation which was only worsened by the government's support for the Manchester magistrates.

The government then passed the Six Acts, a series of measures which seemed very repressive at the time even if they seem less so today. But they were more severe than anything seen up to that time, and among other things they prohibited unauthorised persons from engaging in military exercises, authorised magistrates to issue warrants for searches for arms, and restricted the size of public meetings.

The government had shown itself willing to stamp out disorder. Its firm action against lawlessness, real or imagined, was not matched by measures to alleviate the distress which brought it about. There were some minor reforms, such as the partial abolition of the pillory in 1816, the abolition of the whipping of women in 1820, and, in the previous year, a largely ineffective Factory Act which attempted to place restrictions on the way child labour was used in cotton mills. However, such measures provided no solution to the genuine sufferings of hundreds of thousands of people throughout the country.

b) The Tory Response to Disorder

The government thought of the hardship and misery as being inevitable at a time of social and economic change at the end of a long war. They saw such problems as a feature of the natural working of economic laws and felt that there was nothing they could do to lessen the distress. When Lord Liverpool received a proposal to help commercial undertakings in distressed areas his response reflected this view: 'I am satisfied that government or parliament never meddle with these matters at all but they do harm, more or less'. He often quoted the words of a couplet written by Dr Johnson in the eighteenth century:

How small of all the ills that men endure
The part which Kings or State can cause or cure.

The Home Secretary felt similarly helpless. In his response to a letter asking for some relief for the suffering peoples of Nottinghamshire, he observed: 'I am concerned to think that the prevailing distress is so severely felt in your county, but I see no reason for believing that it would be alleviated by any proceedings at a public meeting or by parliament itself'.

The experience of Birmingham is an instructive one. Distress there was acute, and in 1819 it was estimated that about 27,000 people were 'on relief'. There was a deep-seated loathing of the Corn Laws and the middle and working classes clamoured for parliamentary reform – after all, Birmingham was not separately represented in the House of Commons. In 1818 the distressed artisans sent parliament a piteous plea for help:

1 We, the undersigned, inhabitants of the town of Birmingham, beg leave
  ... to inform you of our forlorn and miserable condition ... We are in
  distress, and in our misery we call upon our country for relief ... We
  ask no more than your honourable House will acknowledge that good
5 citizens have a right to expect. We ask no favour. We only ask to have
  it placed within our power to earn honest bread by honest labour. We
  only ask to be permitted to give our country the benefit of our labour,
  and receive in exchange the scanty comforts necessary for the support
  of life. Our wants are only food and clothing, and shelter from the
10 elements ... Many of us have not had any kind of employment for many
  months, and few of us more than two or three day's work per week, at
  reduced wages ... A general calamity has fallen upon the whole nation,
  and has crushed the happiness of all ... we implore your honourable
  House to remove the cause of misery, whatever it may be. And we
15 cannot but think that your honourable House can remove it. Or if its
  roots are so deeply hidden that no human wisdom can discover them,
  we must then consider them as a visitation from Almighty God, to
  which we must dutifully bend ... we cannot but think that these calami-
  ties originate in natural causes, which it is in the power of human
20 wisdom to discover and remove ... We humbly pray that your
  honourable House will take into consideration our distressed condition, and adopt such measures as in your wisdom may be deemed
  necessary for the relief of ourselves and our suffering country.

The petition seems to have awakened some sympathy within the government. The Chancellor announced that £1m was to be made available for the relief of the poor, to be lent to parish authorities and to be repayable within three years. This illustrates that ministers were not indifferent to the suffering, but they had little idea of what to do about it. Many other people – politicians, economists or writers – did not understand the forces at work. Parliament was lacking in accurate information about the nature and extent of distress, despite the special pleading it heard from groups such as the Birmingham citizenry. Yet even if more had been known, the prevailing *laissez-faire* philosophy of the day did not allow for state action to bring about any improvement.

The government had no answer to distress, but they were clear in their own minds that tension was being exacerbated by Radical orators who exploited the grievances that existed. They suspected that demands for reform would lead to a revolutionary situation, and when they heard tales of the occasional use of tricolours and other emblems of the French Revolutionaries, it only confirmed their worst fears. The language of some of the leaders of popular opinion did suggest that there was reason to be alarmed. James Ings, one of the Cato Street conspirators who aimed to assassinate the Cabinet in 1820, explained his intentions in this way:

1   I will enter the room first. I will go in with a brace of pistols and a knife in my pocket. After the two swordsmen have despatched them, I will cut every head off that is in the room, and Lord Castlereagh's head and Lord Sidmouth's, I will bring away in a bag. For this purpose, I will pro-
5 vide two bags.

Such remarks came only from the wilder fringes of the protesters but they did seem to confirm the Tory analysis. Ministers believed that a radical press and seditious leaders were whipping up the feelings of a 'deluded' people and inciting them to insurrection. They did not think that the mass of people were sufficiently dissatisfied to take action, unless politically motivated agitators were arousing them to protest. They equated any expression of discontent with a threat of revolution and felt that, if Britain was not to go the way that France had gone after 1789 and the whole fabric of society be ruined, strict law and order must be maintained.

The dangers were often much exaggerated and, despite the widespread frustration and alarm, there was little likelihood that Britain would follow the French experience. But demands for reform, when accompanied by any signs of widespread organisation and the threat of violence, made ministers unwilling to take the risk. The government was fearful and uncomprehending. But it was not as sinister or as blindly repressive as radical publicists of the day often claimed. The verdict of the Hammonds,[2] two early twentieth-century historians, overstated the extent of its dictatorial nature: 'Probably no English government has ever been quite so near, in spirit and licence, to the atmosphere that we used to associate with the Tsar's government of Russia'.

In its desire to uphold the traditional way of life of the propertied classes, the government could fairly be charged with self-interest. But in this, of course, they echoed the feelings of the propertied classes throughout the country. In the Pitt Clubs, set up to honour 'the pilot who weathered the storm', feelings ran high against 'malicious' and 'dangerous' extremists, and talk of underground conspiracies was rife. Whigs as well as Tories were alarmed, and Lord Grey on the Whig side was also fearful that the situation would get out of hand. Of the popular leaders he asked: 'Is there one of them with whom you would trust yourself in the dark?'

Eric Evans[3] has stressed how acutely aware ministers were of the danger to the social system at this time. In his view, the French Revolution 'dominated the thinking of an entire generation ...

[Ministers] sincerely believed that that they were fighting to support the old order, hereditary privilege and civilised values against what that quintessentially anti-French Revolutionary warrior Edmund Burke called "rash and speculative opinion" which threatened to destroy the world they knew'. In a period beset by economic and political difficulties, it is unsurprising that they adopted policies with which many libertarians felt ill at ease.

Lacking an effective police force and ultimately reliant on the troops, the government naturally backed the unpaid local magistrates who had the responsibility for maintaining order. Normally members of the landlord class or the clergy, these men feared that the established order was in danger. Ministers felt it was their duty to support them in public, whatever their private doubts. As Canning put it after Peterloo: 'To let down the magistrates would be to invite their resignation and to lose all gratuitous service in the counties liable to distress for ever'.

In his *Lancaster Pamphlet*, John Plowright[4] has defended the performance of the Liverpool administration in its handling of public order issues. His defence relies on three strands, namely that:

i) most popular discontent was not directly attributable to Liverpool's policies, but rather to the impact of the agricultural and industrial revolutions, the population increase and the transition from wartime to peacetime conditions, among other things

ii) although the government may have aggravated unrest, by such means as demobilising troops too quickly and passing the Corn Laws, it did its best to mitigate suffering, for instance by making funds available for public works and other ventures

iii) there were few resources available to ministers, by way of a network of police forces or a sizeable standing army, hence their reliance on informers and agents provocateurs.

Plowright concludes that 'the essential moderation of the government's response is all the more surprising and commendable' in the light of these factors. He sees ministers as having acted with 'commendable restraint', rather than in a repressive way. His evidence includes the fact that many of those who played an important part in the sporadic rioting were not put to death, often having their death sentences commuted to transportation. Others were acquitted by the courts, suggesting that it would be wrong to see the judicial system as playing a key role in carrying out 'repressive' policies, at the behest of ministers.

Gash,[5] whose studies of the era derive mainly from his exhaustive analysis of the career of Sir Robert Peel, takes a similar view. He points out that of those who took part in the Spa Fields riots of 1816 and another in Huddersfield shortly afterwards, most of those who were detained under the suspension of *Habeas Corpus* were released within the year. He observes that this 'was not exactly a reign of terror'.

Derry[6] makes a similar point about the Six Acts which were introduced after Peterloo. He argues that 'what is surprising is not their savagery, but their restraint'.

A thorough modern interpretation of Liverpool and his administration's policies after 1815 has yet to be written. Much recent comment has been more favourable to him, offering the basis of a reasonable defence to the charge that he pursued reactionary policies. He was trying to maintain aristocratic control at a time of social upheaval. He believed that to do so he had to contain working-class discontent by the firm maintenance of law and order. He and others in authority were understandably alarmed by the spate of insurrections and naturally did see these in terms of what had been happening in France a few years before. Their concerns seemed the more justified, given the nature of the radical literature in circulation. Titles such as *The Republican, The Cap of Liberty* and *The Medusa* (the name of a mortal woman in Greek mythology who was transformed into a Gorgon, a hideous winged figure with brazen claws, so monstrous that those who saw her were turned to stone).

c) Economic Toryism

In its economic policy Liverpool's government found itself in disagreement with both the landed and the business classes at different times. The economic situation was central to the post-war difficulties for the problems were of unprecedented severity. The years after Waterloo were bound to be difficult transitional ones as the restoration of peace meant that industries which had flourished in the war found their goods no longer in great demand. At first, the government seemed more sensitive to the position of the landed interest, and the Corn Laws showed the importance they attached to the position of agriculture in the community. Boyd Hilton[7] has shown that ministers were anxious to ensure food supplies and full employment and saw agriculture as the sector most likely to bring these about. Other interests viewed the 1815 laws very differently.

The loss of the anticipated revenue from the Income Tax was a serious blow to national finances and the government found itself with a shortfall of revenue. In 1818 it was running a deficit of £13m and nearly 80 per cent of its revenue was used to pay interest on the National Debt. For the three years after the war no action had been taken to correct the deficit and stabilise the finances because MPs had been unwilling to see measures taken which might have damaged their personal financial well being. They were keen to urge a sharp reduction in expenditure to keep the burden of taxation as low as possible, although there was little the government could do to reduce its level further. There was, as Castlereagh discerned, an 'ignorant impatience of taxation'.

Given the circumstances of acute distress and unpopularity,

Liverpool decided in 1819 that he must make the state of the economy his first priority and take action to restore sound finance. Following the recommendations of a Bullion Committee, which included all senior ministers and was chaired by Sir Robert Peel, the government planned a phased return to the Gold Standard. This meant that in future the £ sterling was to be worth a fixed amount of gold. It was hoped that this would help control the inflation brought about by the banks issuing too many notes (any bank could issue paper money at this time) without having the reserves which would enable them to be converted into gold, on demand. The return to gold did have an effect in checking the rise in prices, and is credited by many economic historians with causing an improvement in Britain's foreign-exchange position and an inflow of gold to the Bank of England.

In that same year, in a more determined attempt to return to solvency, it was proposed in the Budget to collect £3m more in taxes. This was meant to restore confidence, but beyond this goal, Liverpool recognised the crucial need to give a boost to an ailing economy. He wanted to promote a recovery in manufacturing and trade by lowering tariffs. This was a policy which was to be developed in the early 1820s. Ministers came to see that industry rather than agriculture offered the best prospect of economic growth, and the switch in emphasis enabled the government to widen its support by appealing to representatives of industry and commerce whose interests had been sacrificed in 1815.

d) A Ministry Out-Of-Touch with Popular Opinion: the Queen Caroline Affair, 1820

In 1820 the Whigs had an opportunity to embarrass the Tory government when a major political scandal broke out. The new king, George IV, had married Princess Caroline of Brunswick in 1795, but their relationship had long since broken down. Caroline lived a flamboyant and scandalous life abroad. However, when George IV came to the throne she was determined to return to England to be crowned as queen. The king was horrified at such a prospect, and he urged Lord Liverpool to assist him in divorcing his wife. The government decided to begin proceedings, and introduced a Bill in parliament (the only way of gaining a divorce at the time) to dissolve the marriage and thereby deprive her of her desired title.

Such was the display of public support for the 'wronged woman' and so unpopular was George that the Bill had to be withdrawn. Caroline received some support from the Whigs. Among the Tories, Canning was so uneasy at the 'persecution' he thought she was enduring that he resigned from the ministry. Lord Liverpool, who had never wished to be drawn into the affair, got a taste of the public mood when the Bill failed. Amidst much rejoicing in the capital, some ministers had the windows of their homes shattered. Caroline soon faded from public attention (and died a year later) but George's reputation never fully recovered. The government had long been very unpopular and, particularly in 1819–20, it was held in low esteem. Shelley expressed popular feeling in his sonnet, *England*, in which he wrote of 'rulers who neither see, nor feel, nor know'. The gap between government and governed had been growing wider. Peel observed how out of touch with popular opinion the government had become and noted that though the public possessed more influence than ever before. Of a friend he asked:

1 Do you not think that the tone of England . . . is more liberal, to use an odious but intelligible phrase, than the policy of the government? Do not you think that there is a feeling, becoming daily more general and more confirmed . . . in favour of some undefined change in the mode of
5 governing the country?

It required a reconstruction of the government to improve its public image.

3 Liberal Toryism

> **KEY ISSUE** Was there a move away from 'repressive' to 'liberal' Toryism, and if so why did it occur?

The conventional view of Lord Liverpool's premiership is that in 1821–2 his government moved away from a policy of reaction and that this turning point introduced a new era of 'Liberal Toryism' which ran from 1822 to 1827. In the period before the reconstruction of the ministry the 'tough' attitude towards popular discontent and political radicalism, as well as the introduction of the Corn Laws, suggested a government which was primarily determined to defend the position and privileges of the propertied class. The policies of the 1820s, by contrast, seem to mark a thaw. Yet it would be misleading to assume that the ministry consciously changed its outlook in order to introduce a new 'liberal' era.

The change in personnel was a significant one. In January 1822 Peel replaced Sidmouth at the Home Office. Castlereagh, borne down by his labours at the Foreign Office and mercilessly lampooned and abused, broke under the strain and in August 1822 cut his throat with a razor. Canning replaced him in both of his offices. In January 1823 'Prosperity' Robinson replaced Vansittart at the Exchequer and Huskisson became President of the Board of Trade. Some of the old and more reactionary ministers had disappeared, and Canning, Huskisson and Peel, the best-known of the 'new' faces (although they had all served in the Liverpool team in the past), were a welcome addition to the Front Bench in the House of

Commons which had lacked prominent members of the Cabinet previously. After the Queen Caroline affair, the time was ripe for renewal, and the men appointed appeared to be in touch with the spirit of the time. The changes ushered in a more constructive phase in government policy.

However, it is clear that Liverpool was not consciously embarking upon a change of direction. This view is substantiated by the fact that several of the 'new' policies had been introduced or planned before the change of personnel. For example, Wallace, the energetic Vice-President of the Board of Trade, had started on a programme of complete revision of the commercial system and a move towards free trade, although it is Huskisson who is usually credited with the policies of the mid-1820s. But Liverpool's changes in his team created the impression that a more active policy was now to be pursued. The government looked to be more firmly in control of events.

Because there was an improvement in the prevailing economic climate, the government's attitude seemed to change. Widespread unemployment, high prices and 'hunger politics' had created support for radical politics. In the more prosperous climate of the twenties, there was a general state of peace, and the tensions associated with turbulence and unrest subsided as the worst years passed into memory. Against this background, and guided by younger and more able men, the administration was more sympathetic to reform. With the decline in public disturbances, ministers had more time to devote to reconstruction and reform.

Compared with the 'repression' which went before, the policies pursued between 1822 and 1827 seemed more liberal, although it is easy to exaggerate both the extent and the novelty of the changes. They did not immediately harm the interests of the landed backers of the party nor did they conflict with deeply held Tory principles or require heavy expenditure. Nonetheless, important work was done by Peel, Huskisson and Robinson at home, and by Canning abroad, as a brief account of their main measures indicates.

a) Huskisson and Robinson

Over the centuries, tariffs on many imported goods had been introduced in order to protect industry from overseas competition, and others had been added in order to raise money during the wars against revolutionary France. In 1819 a petition from London merchants pleading for an end to these restrictions was presented to parliament. It was received positively by the Liverpool government which was increasingly willing to move along the road towards free trade.

William Huskisson was a rising figure in the Tory Party. He was an enlightened economist and a believer in freer trade. He accepted the view that the more countries traded with each other the richer they would all become. In his words, 'national prosperity will be most effectually promoted by unrestrained competition not only between ... different classes in the same country, but also by extending that competition as much as possible to all countries'.

In the pursuit of these aims, he modified the Navigation Acts which had made it compulsory for all imports to and exports from Britain and the colonies to be carried in English ships or in the ships of the country from which the goods came. From now on ships of all countries could bring in goods. He went further, and lowered some of the duties on goods coming into England, and concluded Reciprocity Treaties with some countries so that there could be a mutually advantageous reduction of tariffs between them.

He was working on a modification of the Corn Laws when he left office, and in this he had the support of Lord Liverpool who had spoken out boldly on agriculture in 1822. Liverpool blamed the post-war distress in the farming community on 'inflation, over-investment and over-production in the war years', and stressed that to bring about recovery it was necessary to see a recovery of the national economy as a whole. He argued that:

> Manufacturing, trade and agriculture are all interdependent, and it is the duty of government and of parliament to hold the balance between all the great interests of the country ... The agricultural is not the only interest in Great Britain. It is not even the most numerous.

The gentry did not like what they heard and were resistant to the prospect of changes in the Corn Laws. Protection was a difficult policy area for Liverpool and other 'liberal' Tories. On the one hand, as followers of Adam Smith, they supported freeing trade from restrictions, believing that this would generate economic growth and widespread prosperity. Free trade would also be in the interests of industry, enabling businessmen to expand and sell their goods abroad, and of consumers too. The public wanted cheaper bread, which would be possible if corn was allowed in from overseas. Against this, ministers knew that there would be strong opposition from many of those who lived and worked in the countryside. In Evans' phrase,[8] the landed interest saw the laws as 'essential props of their survival'. Liverpool did not have to face the opposition encountered in any reforming plans, for he was dead by the time that a sliding scale was put in place, in the lifetime of the Wellington administration.

Huskisson was also the minister involved in the repeal of the Combination Laws, which had been introduced by Pitt in 1800 and 1801 and which had forbidden workers to form trades unions or to organise strikes. Repeal was primarily the work of Francis Place, a Radical tailor who won the support of Joseph Hume, an MP. Hume organised the passage of a Bill in parliament in 1824, and neither Liverpool nor Huskisson fully appreciated the implications of what was being done. After an outbreak of strikes following repeal, the law was modified on the government's instigation in 1825 so that unions were allowed to exist and workers were allowed to strike, but only as long as there was no molestation of workers who did not join.

Overall, Huskisson's economic policy had widened the Tory Party's appeal to include the moderate centre ground. His work between 1822 and 1827 marks him out as a Tory reformer, for he had taken the first significant steps along the road to free trade. Somewhat tragically, he did not live to see many further steps taken, for in 1830 he unwisely stepped in front of a locomotive at the opening ceremony of the Manchester–Liverpool Railway, with fatal results.

Huskisson's work was complemented by that of Robinson at the Exchequer. For a while he presided over a more successful economy, although to a considerable extent this reflected the improvement in trading conditions which had come about since 1819 rather than any action he had taken. At first he was able to balance the budget while reducing taxation. For example, in 1823 there were a number of tax reductions, especially on items likely to be bought by the rich, for Robinson believed that their prosperity would ultimately benefit the whole community. His argument was that if the well-to-do were encouraged to create more wealth, they would then be in a position to take on more workingmen as employees. The concessions were extended to more basic commodities such as coal and wool in the following year, and the Chancellor of the Exchequer was awarded his nickname 'Prosperity Robinson' as a result. When conditions took a turn for the worse in 1825, and a slump in exports caused a deterioration of the national finances, some of the gloss of his reputation wore off.

b) Peel at the Home Office

Sir Robert Peel tackled the savage penal system. Some of the punishments inflicted by the law courts had been most severe and in 1819 alone nearly 10,000 criminals had been transported to Botany Bay in Australia. More than 200 crimes, including pick-pocketing, were punishable by death, but increasingly the penalties did not have the deterrent effect intended. Juries had become reluctant to convict because of the harshness of the law. Often they refused to condemn a person to death for stealing property of little value. Sir Samuel Romilly and Sir James Mackintosh had long campaigned for reform, and Peel took up their ideas so that the death penalty was removed from more than 180 offences and the whole penal system was made more humane. No longer were those who committed suicide to be buried at the crossroads with a stake through their hearts! Mackintosh later commented on the changed situation: 'I could almost think I had lived in two different countries'.

Peel was similarly active in other areas, and in this period the Gaols Act (1823) improved conditions in the insanitary and overcrowded prisons of the larger towns and cities. Regular inspection was to take place and the prisons' administration was to be drastically revised. However, it was the setting up of the Metropolitan Police Force for which Peel is best remembered as Home Secretary. For several years he had been convinced that it was necessary to have a regular police force in London, despite the fears of those who were anxious about a threat to the traditional liberties of Englishmen. He realised that the existing arrangements were grossly inadequate. But it was not until 1829 that he was able to gain enough support for his constructive reform.

Among his other work, Peel worked with Huskisson on the changing status of the trade unions. He supported repeal of the Combination Laws, having been intellectually convinced by the arguments used by those seeking the legalisation of unions. Yet when there was a spate of attacks on strikebreakers he – like other ministers – wanted to see an amendment. His cautious reformism is indicated by his remark that:

1 Men who ... have no property except their manual skills and strength, ought to be allowed to confer together ... for the purpose of determining at what rate they will sell their property. But the possession of such a privilege justified, while it renders more necessary, the severe
5 punishment of any attempt to control the free will of others.

Peel's performance at the Home Office well illustrates the approach of the Liverpool administration in this supposedly more 'liberal' era. As Evans[9] observes: 'Nowhere in the final phase of Liverpool's government is the emphasis on continuity rather than change between the 1780s and the 1820s more apt than in the stewardship ... of Sir Robert Peel. Like Pitt, Peel was more effective as an administrator and codifier, than as an innovator'. His changes, when they came, were not the product of his own thinking, for he rarely had novel ideas himself. However, he did excel in translating the ideas of others into practical effect. He listened well and was open to persuasion. And despite being immersed in administrative detail, he supported the work of Huskisson and Robinson, in their 'economic' changes.

It had been Peel's ambition to bequeath 'some record of the trust I have held which may outlive the fleeting discharge of the mere duties of ordinary routine, and that may perhaps confer some distinction on my name, by connecting it with permanent improvements in the judicial institutions of the country'. He had proceeded cautiously, for he feared that too hasty an approach might have created a 'strong prejudice ... against measures that were intended for the public good; and thus the great object of justice and humanity might be defeated'. It may be that, as Beales suggests,[10] his main concern was to make the workings of the law more rational rather than more merciful, and that the beneficial effects of his improvements can be overstated. But for a Tory Home Secretary, operating at a time when more traditionally minded party supporters had a deep respect for every aspect of the existing legal system, the work accomplished was for-ward-looking and highly significant. In ridding it of anomalies and injustices, he was making it function better.

By his willingness to reform, Peel was making it more likely that the essentials of society as he knew it could be preserved. By his mastery of his case and the measured and reasoned style of his exposition, he was winning for himself almost universal respect within the House. Members were impressed by the professionalism of his performances. Here was a man of powerful intellect, with a remarkable capacity for hard work and a willingness to grapple with difficult problems and issues.

c) Canning at the Foreign Office, 1822–7

George Canning was the Tory held in the highest popular esteem, and during his period as Foreign Secretary British policy took on a more liberal tinge. He was disliked by the reactionary clique of states-men who governed in Europe, and gained a reputation as the enemy of kings and the friend of peoples. This was partly because of his work in supporting the cause of liberty and constitutionalism in Greece, Portugal and Spain, but particularly because of his backing for the freedom and independence of the South American republics which were in the process of breaking away from the Spanish empire. Gladstone was later to describe him as the first English friend of peo-ples struggling for their freedom. The historian H.A.L. Fisher[11] was similarly impressed by his achievements, and concluded that 'he was in foreign policy an exponent of the new type of popular and liberal diplomacy'.

Canning's emphasis on the 'Englishness' of his approach and his willingness to ignore the niceties of diplomacy went down well with many people. His attitude and manner, and his attempt to make foreign policy popular and intelligible, made him seem more pro-gressive than he was. A glance at his record in home affairs casts some doubt on the reality of his liberalism. True, he did support Catholic Emancipation, but he had also defended the magistrates at Peterloo in remarks that could have come from the mouth of Lord Sidmouth, and he had supported the Six Acts. He also opposed any reform of the criminal law and of the electoral system,

Yet for all of the limitations of his views on domestic policy, his presence in the government was reassuring to those who wanted to see reform. He was highly intelligent and had shrewdly cultivated public opinion. The Whig Lord Brougham (pronounced 'Broom') noted one useful gift that he possessed: 'He was an actor, a first-rate one no doubt, but still an actor'. He had the 'gift of the gab', and could sell his policies. He contrived to take credit for any of the gov-ernment's reforms that were popular, whilst detaching himself from the odium of any that were less pleasing.

d) The End of the Liverpool Ministry

In February 1827 Liverpool resigned following a stroke. He died a year later. His reputation had often been attacked, and literary radicals such as Byron and Shelley condemned his government in the years immediately after 1815 as reactionary and repressive. Such terms are still used by some historians today – if only to provide a contrast with the approach to government in the 1820s.

Those on the political Left are apt to stress the sinister use of police spies and *agents provocateurs*, the lack of any real attempt to relieve distress, and the government's reactions to the tragedy of Peterloo. Those on the Right tend to concentrate more on the difficulties in which the government found itself and to show that in their attitudes they were representative of the thinking men of their time. They stress that ministers were dealing with problems of immense complexity, including those of a nascent industrial society at the end of a long war.

In his dated, but still highly regarded, study of Lord Liverpool, Brock[12] noted that the Prime Minister was

ı representative of his age in a way that few statesmen have been, for he
  reflected both its prejudices and its enlightenment in exact proportions
  ... He seems, at one moment, to be looking back to the eighteenth century, at another to have set his face towards the prosperous commer-
5 cial world of the nineteenth century.

Throughout his premiership he pursued a conservative policy which was to provide the basis for the new Conservative Party of Sir Robert Peel – a moderate coalition of those who favoured cautious reform combined with a strong defence of law and order. To judge him only by his response to radical discontent is to ignore his more constructive approach, especially after 1819, in economic policy and the other changes in domestic policy over which he presided in the 1820s. The true measure of his achievement as a party leader was to become more apparent after his passing from the scene, when his conciliatory gifts were much missed and no one else could maintain harmony between the various personalities and factions within the Tory Party.

e) The Break-up of Liberal Toryism

On Liverpool's death George IV invited Canning to become Prime Minister. Several High Tories (and Peel, who disagreed with Canning over Catholic Emancipation) immediately resigned from the government so that the new Prime Minister had to include some Whigs in his ministry in order to fill all the vacancies. In 1827 he was widely admired, respected by many as a genuine liberal, and his government was perhaps the most enlightened in tone for 20 years. However, Canning was not in office long enough to tackle the major issue of the time – the Catholic problem – for by August of the same year he was dead.

Robinson, now known as Lord Goderich, briefly succeeded Canning, and this intelligent and popular man headed a government similar in composition to that of its predecessor. As a Prime Minister Goderich was weak and easily bullied by his colleagues, whom he could not control. He even broke down in the act of offering to resign. George proffered his pocket handkerchief and accepted the resignation.

By comparison, his successor, the Duke of Wellington, was a 'strong' man. His administration included Peel back at the Home Office and for a while the Canningites remained. Eventually, after a wrangle concerning redistribution of parliamentary seats, the more reforming elements, including Huskisson, resigned in 1828. Technically their resignation marks the end of the era of Liberal Toryism for some of the more progressive Tories such as Lord Palmerston, who had held minor office since 1809, went over to the Whig side to lay the foundations of the nineteenth-century Liberal Party.

4 The Demise of 'Church and King Toryism'

> **KEY ISSUES** In what ways did the Wellington leadership show itself to be willing to embrace necessary reform? In what ways was it out-of-touch with the needs of the time?

a) Wellington as Prime Minister, 1828–30

After the exit of the 'progressives', much depended on Wellington and Peel. The Duke was a stubborn man of narrow vision and little intellectual consistency. His speeches were those of a High Tory who believed that the British constitution was perfect. Yet he had a strong sense of duty and his devotion to the nation's welfare was unquestionable. He was ultimately willing to adapt his policy to bring it in line with the needs of the day, for he usually knew when the time had come to give way.

His ministry accomplished some useful changes, notably the establishment of the Metropolitan Police. However, it soon fell to Wellington's government to deal with the Catholic question and this issue wrecked any remaining unity within the Tory Party. The prelude to Emancipation was the passage of a bill which repealed the Test and Corporations Act with respect to Protestant Dissenters (Non-conformists). In reality, this particular law had been a dead letter for a long time, for they had been able to assume public office and take a parliamentary seat for many years. However, this tidying-up measure was watched with interest by Roman Catholics because their disabilities were never likely to be removed as long as Dissenters were, in theory at least, bound by similar restrictions.

The government was in an acute dilemma over the Catholic question. Daniel O'Connell had been elected as MP for County Clare in Ireland but, because he was a Roman Catholic, he was unable to take his seat at Westminster. There was much excitement and the prospect of violent disorder throughout Ireland if O'Connell were to be permanently denied the right to serve as an MP. The situation would be even worse if at the next election more Catholics were returned and were similarly debarred. Wellington had consistently endorsed a strongly Protestant position and had been opposed to any measure of Catholic Emancipation, but with aristocratic pessimism he was now prepared to give way in the current circumstances. Peel was in a more difficult position. He had been a passionate and unbending opponent of Emancipation, to which he had ably led much of the opposition. He would have preferred to leave the government so that Emancipation could be introduced by those who either really believed in it, or at least were less hostile to it than he was. However, he had a strong sense of loyalty to the Prime Minister and was persuaded by him to remain in office.

There was no halfway house on this question. The government must either resist Irish pressure, with all the attendant dangers of so doing, or accept the reality of the situation and bring in repeal. In 1829 Peel introduced the measure in the House of Commons, and Wellington used his influence in the Lords to persuade colleagues to relent in their opposition. In both chambers there was a massive revolt against the leadership, with 198 MPs and 116 Peers voting against the party line. Nonetheless, as a result of their effort, Catholic Emancipation was passed. In the process Peel's reputation suffered a grievous blow for, along with Wellington, he was accused of betraying the Tory Party. However, he felt that he was acting appropriately:

1 The events of the Clare election [when O'Connell was elected], with the conviction that the same scenes would be enacted in nearly every county in Ireland if matters were to remain just as they have been for the last five or six years, convinced me that it was not safe for the
5 Protestant interest in Ireland that they should remain so.

His critics were unimpressed by his stance and alleged that he had changed his name from 'R. Peel to Repeal'. As far as they were concerned he had clung onto office despite abandoning the firm principles he had consistently espoused. They believed that, in clinging to office, he was sacrificing Tory principles to personal ambition. On this occasion he was able to survive the growing suspicion of him, but he was to be unable to repeat this success when another issue came up in his career which posed the same question – whether it is appropriate in politics to change one's mind on an important issue and yet to remain in office (see pages 61–8).

A few months later the ministry fell when all of its enemies lined up against it. The Tories were in disarray and in no position to survive a critical vote in the House, for they were hopelessly divided. There were by this time three broad groups within the party:

1. the remaining ex-Canningites, a more progressive group on the left, who did not, however, always act in unison;
2. the centre, which followed Peel and Wellington, and accepted the inevitability of moderate and reasonable change;
3. the Ultras who opposed change of any kind.

So large was the group of Ultras that according to Frank O'Gorman[13] it constituted 'a party within a party'. It had the sympathy of the king and the Tory press, and was attempting to 'convert the all-inclusive Toryism of Liverpool, Peel and Wellington into a narrow, coherent, well-organised and popularly-supported anti-reform Tory party'.

However, those on the Tory side who had up until then opposed parliamentary reform were losing their cohesion. Whilst the bulk of the party rejected any change in the electoral system, some believed that a more representative House of Commons would have never allowed the passage of Catholic Emancipation and were therefore prepared to support a moderate measure of reform.

b) Parliamentary Reform and the 1832 Act

In 1830 the Whigs took office. When a Reform Bill was introduced, the Tories opposed the measure. This was because, whereas the Whigs felt that in the excited circumstances of the time some repair-work to the constitution was necessary, the Tories mostly thought that such a change was definitely not required. Ultras opposed it outright, for they disapproved of almost all reform on principle and believed that further concessions must inevitably be for the worse. Less extreme Tories saw dangers in parliamentary reform because they felt that it would disturb the balance of the constitution. Peel shared this view. His anxiety was that any measure of reform would ultimately lead to Britain becoming a democratic state based on universal franchise, as a door would be opened which, once ajar, would be impossible to close again.

The Whig proposals were not dramatically far-reaching, but on their publication one Tory speaker introduced a theme which was to be endlessly repeated. He claimed that the bill was 'a revolution that will overturn all the natural influence of rank and property'. Other points were added subsequently. The proposed reform was seen as an exercise in 'robbery and pillage' in that it threatened private property by eliminating those boroughs which were controlled by landed patrons. It was argued that it would transfer power from the gentry to the industrial classes, for 'the field of coal would beat the field of barley', and that it would introduce a system in which there were just as many anomalies as before. Above all, however, there was the fear that this reform would be followed by more reform, and that the innovations would not just affect the electoral system, but that they would ultimately change other institutions as well. Thus the monarchy, the Lords, the Church, and private property were claimed to be under threat as well. As one critic put it, 'all will be levelled to the plane of the petty shopkeeper and small farmer'.

Whatever the merits of the Tory case, it did not meet the needs of the immediate situation. It was true that this measure could never be a final measure, but in 1832 some reform was a practical necessity – just as Catholic Emancipation had been in 1829. The new voters endorsed the Whig bill when it became law in 1832, for in December of that year they gave the party a large majority, and inflicted on the Tories their worst defeat in the nineteenth century.

c) The Direction of Toryism, 1815–32

The years between 1815 and 1832 were significant ones in the history of the Tory Party. After Liverpool's retirement the party seriously split as it encountered a number of contentious issues. The dilemma of many conservatives came to the surface in their reaction to them. Should they bow to the inevitable when changes were needed, or should they fight in the last ditch to defend their principles and position? Might reform lead to revolution, or was it the case that acceptance of reform when the time was prudent would stave off catastrophe?

There were many Tories, such as Lord Eldon, who favoured fighting a rearguard action and who could not stand the approach of those who bent with the wind and made concessions. However, it was the Liverpools, the Huskissons and the Peels, or those like them in attitude, who dominated the Party's direction and had responsibility for its strategy. They ensured that conservatives knew when it was time to adapt to the needs and realities of the time.

d) Tory Party Organisation

Until 1832 Tory Party organisation, even within Parliament, was of a very basic kind. Few people were involved. Policies and tactics were the preserve of the great men in the party, and the leaders rarely met with their supporters. Occasionally, there were meetings of Tory MPs at which the leaders might explain their thinking or strategy, or more likely plead for better attendance. They might also try to inspire and enthuse their supporters, in the hope of winning them over to their viewpoint, although some leaders saw no necessity to do so.

Apart from regular parliamentary life at Westminster, there were many informal gatherings in clubs and private houses where political discussion could and did take place. Thoughts on the issues of the day would be exchanged over the dining tables of fashionable houses, where grandees who were not in parliament could make their views known.

Political parties did not extend to the country at large, for organisation was unnecessary at a time when so few people had the vote. However, there were a number of societies which had been established to perpetuate the memory of past heroes. In particular, the Pitt Clubs preserved the memory of William Pitt the Younger, and idealised his performance and achievement. After Waterloo, members were strident in their demands for tough government action and strong sentences from the magistrates. The cult remained for several years, and dinners, anniversaries and the production of numerous biographies and portraits kept the memory alive.

The local picture of party activity is a confusing one. In some areas, such as Hampshire, there had been candidates using the party names of Whig and Tory as far back as 1806–7. O'Gorman[13] has shown that in about half of the English counties, party labels were being employed in the 1820s. Activity was often not continuous, and it was purely local in inspiration. It tended to increase in times of political excitement, as in the years 1829–32. Again, within the boroughs, there is no clear-cut pattern. In many boroughs the labels were only used occasionally. Even then the causes espoused bore little relation to what was being said and done nationally. In a minority of boroughs, there was regular party rivalry, as at Lichfield where two local families dominated affairs, one on each side of the political divide. In a very few larger boroughs there was more marked activity in which either side identified more closely with the views expressed by representatives at Westminster.

O'Gorman concluded his survey of the scene before the Reform Act by saying that:

1 Few constituencies were without their clubs and societies, their rituals and their calendars of birth-dates, anniversaries and celebrations. These clubs were the local agencies of party organisation before central party institutions reached out to touch the constituencies ... Some, a min-
5 ority, used the words 'Whig' and 'Tory'. Others used the ... terminology of colours, the Yellows v the Blues of Ipswich, for example. In others, the enigmatic 'Constitutional Club' might find itself in conflict with the 'Independent Club'.

References

1 R. Blake, *The Conservative Party from Peel to Major* (Heinemann, 1997)
2 J. and B. Hammond, *The Town Labourer* (Guild Books, 1925, reissued 1949)
3 E. Evans, *Britain before the Reform Act: Politics and Society 1815–1832* (Longman, 1989)
4 J. Plowright, 'Regency England: the Age of Lord Liverpool', *Lancaster Pamphlet* (Routledge, 1996)

5   N. Gash, *Lord Liverpool* (Weidenfeld, 1984)
6   J. Derry, *Politics in the Age of Fox, Pitt and Liverpool* (Macmillan, 1990)
7   Boyd Hilton, *Corn, Cash, Commerce: The Economic Policies of the Tory Governments of 1815–30* (OUP, 1977)
8   E. Evans, 'Sir Robert Peel: Statesmanship, Power and Party', *Lancaster Pamphlet* (Routledge, 1991)
9   E. Evans, 'Sir Robert Peel: Statesmanship, Power and Party', *Lancaster Pamphlet*
10 D. Beales, 'Peel, Russell and Reform', *The Historical Journal*, 1974
11 H. Fisher, *A History of Europe* (Eyre and Spottiswoode, 1935)
12 W. Brock, *Lord Liverpool and Liberal Toryism* (Cambridge, 1941)
13 F. O'Gorman, *The Emergence of the British Two Party System 1760–1832* (Edward Arnold, 1990)

Summary
The Age of Lord Liverpool and Beyond, 1815–32

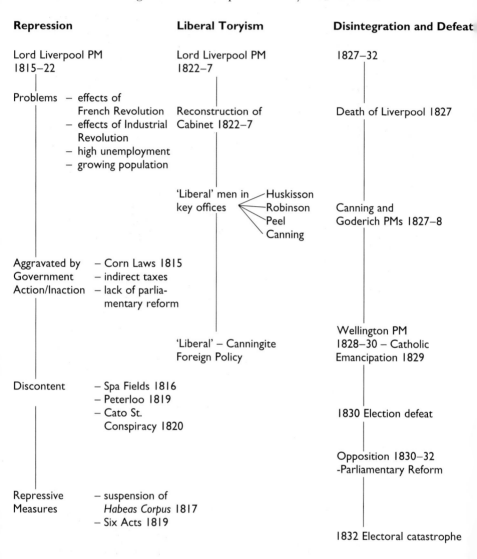

Repression

Lord Liverpool PM
1815–22

Problems — effects of
French Revolution
— effects of Industrial
Revolution
— high unemployment
— growing population

Aggravated by
Government
Action/Inaction
— Corn Laws 1815
— indirect taxes
— lack of parlia-
mentary reform

Discontent
— Spa Fields 1816
— Peterloo 1819
— Cato St.
Conspiracy 1820

Repressive
Measures
— suspension of
Habeas Corpus 1817
— Six Acts 1819

Liberal Toryism

Lord Liverpool PM
1822–7

Reconstruction of
Cabinet 1822–7

'Liberal' men in
key offices
— Huskisson
— Robinson
— Peel
— Canning

'Liberal' — Canningite
Foreign Policy

Disintegration and Defeat

1827–32

Death of Liverpool 1827

Canning and
Goderich PMs 1827–8

Wellington PM
1828–30 – Catholic
Emancipation 1829

1830 Election defeat

Opposition 1830–32
-Parliamentary Reform

1832 Electoral catastrophe

Working on Chapter 2

Read the second paragraph of the 'Points to Consider' section at the beginning of the chapter.

Think out how you are going to arrange your notes on this chapter. If you follow the advice given in 'Points to Consider' you will start by compiling a list of the main political events between 1815 and 1827 under the headings 'Repressive (1815–22)' and 'Liberal (1822–7)'. Include enough details about each event so that they will remind you of other things you have read when you use your notes during revision.

Your second task will be to draw up a short two-column table headed 'Change and Continuity, 1815–27'. In the first column list as many things as you can think of that changed in British politics during this time. In the second column list elements of political life which did not change. Decide whether there was more change or more continuity.

Thirdly, make as many numbered points as you can under the heading 'The Tories in 1827'. Lastly, construct a short chronological table under the heading 'What Happened to the Tories, 1827–30'.

Answering structured and essay questions on Chapter 2

As you probably already know, one of the most important techniques to learn when preparing to answer structured questions is the making of an accurate assessment of exactly what you are required to do when tackling each part of the question. If you can do this, you are likely to score the best mark that could be gained by whatever knowledge and understanding you have. Look at the three-part question below.

a) What problems faced Lord Liverpool's government in the five years following the battle of Waterloo in 1815?

b) How well did the government deal with these problems?

c) Why did some of the government's policies change after 1822?

Two of these questions basically require you to make a list. Which one asks for something different? When you are asked 'How well' it is always expected that you will explain different points of view. Of course, you should say what you think and why you think it but, on its own, that will never attract high marks. Whenever making a historical judgment you must show an awareness of that there are worthwhile interpretations other than the one you have chosen.

Essay questions on the Tories between 1815 and 1830 are often of the 'compare and contrast/similarities and differences/continuity and change' type of question. It is worthwhile you planning your work on this topic with this possibility firmly in mind. Examine the essay questions below.

1. What, if anything, changed in the approach and policies of Lord Liverpool's government in the early 1820s?
2. Why did the Tory Party largely disintegrate between 1827 and 1830?
3. Compare and contrast the problems faced by Lord Liverpool's government in the years after Waterloo and in the 1820s.
4. 'The period 1815–30 was one of continuity rather than change in British political life.' Discuss.

Three of these questions are of the same general type. Which one is the odd one out? If possible, it is best always to include differing points of view or interpretations in an essay answer. However, it would be the exceptional candidate who was able to follow this advice when answering question 2) or question 3). Can you think of any way of answering these questions which involves giving more than one point of view?

Source-based questions on Chapter 2

1. *The Plea of the Birmingham Artisans*
Read the comments of Lord Liverpool on page 25 and the Birmingham artisans' petition on page 26 and answer the following questions:

a) What were the problems faced by the distressed artisans of Birmingham in 1818? (*3 marks*)
b) What are the artisans hoping to achieve by this petition? (*2 marks*)
c) Noting the comments attributed to Lord Liverpool how would he be likely to respond to the Birmingham petition? (*5 marks*)
d) Examine the view that Lord Liverpool's government was, from 1815 to 1822, faced with problems for which it could provide no solutions other than repression (*15 marks*)

2. *The Unpopularity of Liverpool's Government*
Read the poem on page 22 and the speech of the Cato Street conspirator on page 27 and answer the following questions:

a) Why, in your opinion was the conspirator, James Ings particularly keen to have the heads of Castlereagh and Sidmouth? (*3 marks*)
b) How highly should a historian studying the period 1815 to 1822 value Shelley's poem as historical evidence? (*7 marks*)
c) In the light of these two extracts and the plea of the Birmingham artisans on page 9 consider how justified the government was in seeing the country as on the brink of revolution. (*15 marks*)

3 The Primacy of Peel, 1832–46

POINTS TO CONSIDER

In 1835, Peel committed the Tories to acceptance of the 1832 Reform Act which they had opposed at the time of its passing. He understood that the party must change and broaden its appeal, if it was to win the support of the newly-enfranchised voters. With this in mind, the milder word 'Conservative' was used, instead of 'Tory'. The refashioning of the Conservative Party was not carried out without imposing considerable strain on his followers, many of whom were resistant to his modernising tendencies. On a series of issues, particularly after the party gained office in 1841, he and they were at odds. Matters came to a head over the repeal of the Corn Laws, when the young Benjamin Disraeli emerged as his most effective tormentor.

In this chapter, you need to be aware of three aspects of Peel's performance: his creation of the new Conservative party, his reforms between 1841 and 1846, and the developing tensions between him and more right wing MPs. When you have considered his work, you will be in a position to assess his contribution to the party and to the country at large.

KEY DATES

1832	Passage of First Reform Act: Conservatives in disarray.
1834–5	Peel briefly Prime Minister.
1835	Publication of Tamworth Manifesto.
1835–41	Creation of the modern Conservative Party.
1841	Conservatives won election.
1841–6	Peel and the Conservatives back in office.
1845–6	Controversy over repeal of the Corn Laws: Peel's downfall.
1850	Peel died.

1 Creating the New Conservative Party

> **KEY ISSUES** What was 'new' in Peel's new Conservative Party? To whom did it primarily appeal?

a) The Situation in 1832

The Tory Party went out of office in 1830 and two years later it suffered one of the most shattering defeats in its history – it was reduced to a rump of 185 MPs. Even in the counties, traditionally a stronghold of Conservatism, years of agricultural depression had taken their toll, and the party won only 42 of the 144 seats. Most of its support came

A Note on ... use of the term 'Conservative'

By 1830 the term had been used sporadically over several years. It was of continental origin. Its use was usually in the French form, as when Wellington spoke in 1827 of the 'parti conservateur' in the country. Three years later an anonymous writer in the *Quarterly Review* noted that: 'We now are, as we always have been, decidedly and conscientiously attached to what is called the Tory, and which might with more propriety be called, the Conservative Party'.

By December 1831 the *Standard* (a daily newspaper) was using 'Conservative' as if it was widely understood, and certainly between 1830 and 1832 it was more frequently used as the label to denote those who stood for the conservation of ancient British institutions. However, it was only after the Reform Act that the word 'Conservative' entered into regular use. Its adoption by politicians and writers was a deliberate attempt to purge the party of its old associations and the change implied a modest alteration of direction. The word 'Tory' had some odious connections. It was a reminder of the dark days after 1815, of the Peterloo massacre, and of governments which had seemed to be dedicated to the defence of privilege and property rather than to the good of the country as a whole. Now was the time to broaden the party's appeal and to reach out to a wider section of the community. 'Conservative' had a milder nuance, suggesting the preservation of the best of the past, whilst in no way implying absolute hostility to reform.

To be seen as an anti-reformer after 1832 was unlikely to do much for one's electoral prospects. True, some more elderly supporters did still like to be thought of as good, old-fashioned Tories. For example, it was the king's brother, the Duke of Cumberland, who remarked in 1830 that, 'Any change, at any time, is highly to be deprecated'. Peel viewed things differently. For him, Conservatism should 'be compatible with cautious and well-digested reforms in every institution which really requires reform, and with redress of proven grievances'.

As such, the new name stressed the need for political and social stability to protect society from 'that bloody anarchy striding towards us'. It would appeal to those 'responsible' elements who wished to defend the constitution from subversion and to resist dangerous and radical encroachments. Yet it would also enable the party to pursue the path of cautious reform.

from the smaller boroughs of less than 1,000 voters. The Tories won in only 8 of the larger urban constituencies. The expanded electorate had rewarded the Whigs for their willingness to concede parliamentary reform and had punished the Tories for their flat refusal to entertain it. The Tories had been humiliated. They now needed to find a way of attracting the voters who had been enfranchised by the 1832 Act. In England and Wales it was only the middle classes who had been given the vote so it was to them that the party had to broaden its appeal. It was to do this on the basis of Conservatism, rather than on the basis of Toryism which was identified in the public mind with absolute hostility to reform.

When the first reformed parliament met in 1832 there was no recognised Conservative leader. As an ex-prime minister, Wellington was still a key figure, politically active in the House of Lords. However, he had made it clear that he was not interested in resuming the premiership. Peel was undoubtedly the leading Conservative in the House of Commons but some discontented Ultras had reservations about formally accepting him as their leader. It was not until the political crisis of 1834, when the king dismissed Lord Melbourne as Prime Minister, that Peel's position was settled beyond any doubt. On Wellington's advice, William IV sent for Peel and asked him to form a government. He was to guide the party for more than a decade, with responsibility for both its policy and its parliamentary tactics. He was indisputably the man in charge and only a major revolt would have pitched him out. He exercised great influence on his parliamentary party, determined the general direction in which it moved and re-united supporters in the House of Commons. He provided the drive and was aware that the future of the party was, in Briggs's phrase,[1] 'bound up in him'.

b) Peel's Personality

'A constitutional statesman is, in general, a man of common opinions and uncommon abilities'. So wrote the nineteenth-century political commentator Walter Bagehot with reference to Sir Robert Peel. The description is a very appropriate one, for if his views were unremarkable, often the product of other men's ideas, his personal qualities were in many ways outstanding. Bagehot was not an uncritical admirer of Peel, finding many aspects of his outlook distasteful, but the remark emphasises the pre-eminence of the man. Peel was undoubtedly the dominant Conservative, indeed the dominant politician, of his age. His career symbolised the acceptance of the new men made possible by the growth of manufacturing: '[it] meant the replacement of a class born to rule by men whose own effort constituted their title to place'. The Peels were middle class. By instinct and background, Peel was a product of the Industrial Revolution. His father, a firm, domineering Conservative, had made a fortune as a mill owner, and the advantages of wealth meant that the son could benefit from the best education that money could buy.

If Peel began with advantages, he climbed to the top because of his ability. Like his father he was very industrious. He was a model son who wished to live up to his family's high expectations of him. He was honest and determined, and used his obvious talents to the full. He was educated at Harrow, where he was a friend of the future poet and romantic, Byron, and then at Oxford University, where the two men were again contemporaries. As students they were of highly contrasting style. One had flair, imagination and spontaneous impulses. The other, the future prime minister, was shy, withdrawn and intelligent in a methodical sort of way; he worked with continuous application. As Byron later put it: 'I was always in scrapes, Peel never'. Peel was the first student to gain a double first in Maths and Classics, an achievement of outstanding merit. As much of the work was examined orally, before an audience as well as the examiners, it was a daunting experience for all concerned. It required a fine memory, a sharp mind and great clarity of expression. These were just the attributes which Peel possessed.

In his adult life those qualities of his youth remained with Peel. His industry, his mastery of a mass of even complex material, his great understanding and common sense, were apparent to all who knew him, as was his unquestionable integrity. Lord Sidmouth, once a colleague and latterly an opponent, paid tribute to that 'great, powerful, laborious intellect, that unflinching diligence'. Disraeli, who found some aspects of his manner distasteful, noted that 'he was gifted with the faculty of method in the highest degree; and with great powers of application which were sustained by a prodigious memory'. But Peel's was not a fertile or constructive mind; rather, it was essentially practical, concerned with the pressing circumstances and preoccupied with the details of the case. Disraeli went on to observe that:

1 Thus gifted and thus accomplished, Sir Robert Peel had a great
   deficiency; he was without imagination ... No one was more sagacious
   when dealing with the circumstances before him; no one penetrated the
   present with more acuteness and accuracy. His judgement was faultless,
5 provided he had not to deal with the future.

It was a mind of narrow range, interested in the techniques of application rather than the discovery of principle. As one writer put it,[1] 'the passion for perfection of detail tended to make him more interested in the way in which a thing was done than in the larger aspects of the thing he was doing'.

Most who knew him found him aloof and cold, which led the Irish MP Daniel O'Connell to compare his smile to the gleam on the silver plate of a coffin lid. Lord Ashley, who never got on with him, found him 'like an iceberg, with a slight thaw on the surface'. His manner was awkward, for he was shy by nature. He only felt at ease in the formal setting of the House of Commons or in the companionship of his family. Many found him humourless, but he could laugh heartily, for example, as he recounted a bawdy story with a group of young and close associates. They found him warm and considerate, and after his death the Duke of Newcastle claimed that he 'could never take a step in public life without reflecting how he [Peel] would have thought of it'. Gladstone was even more complimentary: 'Taken all round, he was the greatest man I have ever known'.

Significantly, after his death he commanded even more respect than when he was alive. By then the less comfortable features of his personality could be more easily overlooked. He was not an easy man. He had a fiery temper, sometimes described as 'peppery'. He was proud and sensitive, and easily wounded by attacks on him. He was often egotistical, given to employing the first person as he laid down what he thought was the appropriate line to take. This made him often overbearing, and he could be a prig. He was convinced of his own rightness, and believed that if something had to be done, then probably he was the best man to do it. He was regarded, even by party supporters, with a degree of suspicion. He never sought to win them round, a trait which was to leave him dangerously exposed in the more difficult moments of his career. More conciliation and charm in such times would have done him a power of good. His manner often seemed to increase the antagonism of those whom he led.

In the House of Commons he was relaxed, and as a speaker he had considerable gifts. He never lost traces of his Lancashire accent, but he had worked to overcome his lack of confidence on social occasions and to achieve self-control. So convincing was his performance that Disraeli could say that Peel's voice was one of the two most perfect things he had ever known – which makes one wonder what the other was! He was a skilful debater, and if he rarely reached the heights of impassioned oratory, he even more rarely produced an unworthy performance. He was masterly in expounding a case, and his speeches could sway the outcome of a debate, though he persuaded men less by the quality of his argument than by the brilliance of the manner in which it was stated. Disraeli had doubts about his performance as party leader but two years after his death could pronounce him to have been 'the greatest Member of Parliament that ever lived'.

c) The Road to Recovery

Peel accepted that the 1832 Reform Act was irreversible, and that his party must learn to live with it. He recognised that old-fashioned attitudes were doomed to failure and that the Tories needed to broaden their appeal to attract moderate opinion, especially that of the industrial middle classes. He saw that there was nothing to be gained from clinging to the attitudes of the Wellingtonian era. Some of his landowning supporters would have liked to put the clock back to the situation before the extension of the franchise, and stayed loyal to the old policy of 'Protectionism, Protestantism and No Popery'. This would have done nothing to attract middle-of-the-road voters, and would have left the Tories as a narrow-based, largely aristocratic rump, destined for eventual oblivion.

Peel's first speech to the reformed parliament committed him to an acceptance of the Reform Act and to the need for gradual reform. It was a fine performance which showed his pre-eminence on the Opposition side of the House. He seemed to be a figure around whom some Tories and many more moderate Conservatives might rally. He was less pessimistic about future prospects than the Duke of Wellington, and his performance and outlook helped to build up party morale. It was now his task to create a new party from the wreckage of 1832. This presented him with a serious problem of leadership, for some of the younger and more progressive members of the Tory Party had gone over to the Whig side in 1830, whilst on the traditional wing he was viewed with distrust and hostility because of his change of mind over Catholic Emancipation.

Out of the disarray on his backbenches, he needed to rebuild party strength by reconstructing the old Tory Party into a new and more appealing creation. The theme was to be moderate reform within the spirit of the constitution. This was a position which would appeal to that section of the community, as yet not Conservative, which was anxious about the threat of disorder and dangerous radical innovation, but which was well-disposed to peaceful change when this seemed appropriate. The king's dismissal of the Melbourne government in 1834 was to give a boost to the Conservative Party, and launch it on the road to recovery. As we have seen, it established Peel's supremacy over his colleagues and made him not only party leader but also prime minister. His government was in a minority, and consequently was only short-lived. After a series of parliamentary defeats, he asked the king to dissolve parliament and to hold an election in January 1835. For this, he took the opportunity to explain his new, milder Conservatism in an address to the voters.

d) The *Tamworth Manifesto*

Although Peel wrote the manifesto to his own constituents, he was really addressing the electorate at large. Copies of the seven-page document were sent to the London newspapers, and on publication there was an immediate reaction in the political world, where the manifesto provoked enormous interest. In the past, governments had occasionally listed their achievements in a document, but there had been nothing comparable to this declaration of principles on the eve of an election. As such, the *Tamworth Manifesto* was a publication without parallel, and its importance in establishing the tone of the Conservative Party was immense. Here was the basis for the new

Conservatism, although neither the creed nor the party were mentioned by name. Peel asserted the need for strong government and the preservation of existing institutions, but combined this with an acceptance that the Reform Act was 'a final and irrevocable settlement of a great constitutional question'. He pledged a future Conservative government to review institutions without infringing on established rights, and to tackle proven abuses. He appealed to his earlier record as a minister to show that he had never supported the continuation of 'acknowledged evils', nor been 'the enemy of judicious reforms'. He wrote:

1 Then as to the spirit of the Reform Bill, and the willingness to adopt and enforce it as a rule of government. If by adopting the spirit of the Reform Bill it be meant that we are to live in a perpetual vortex of agitation that public men can only support themselves in public estimation
5 by adopting every popular impression of the day, by promising the instant redress of anything which anybody may call an abuse, by abandoning altogether that great aid of government, more powerful than either law or reason, the respect for ancient rights, and the deference to prescriptive authority; if this be the spirit of the Reform Bill, I will not
10 undertake to adopt it; but if the spirit of the Reform Bill implies merely a careful review of institutions, civil and ecclesiastical, undertaken in a friendly temper, combining, with the firm maintenance of established rights, the correction of proved abuses, and the redress of real grievances, in that case I can, for myself and my colleagues, undertake to act
15 in such a spirit, and with such intentions.

This was a bold bid for the middle ground. Such attitudes were likely to strike a response in all those reasonable men who wanted effective government accompanied by judicious reform. It seemed a wise position to take, accepting the irreversibility of what had been done but not proceeding too rapidly along the road marked 'reform'. Landowners and bourgeoisie could unite in the defence of property, but by conceding the need for some further changes there was a likelihood of wider support. Gash[2] neatly encapsulated the purpose of Peel's endeavour in his observation that the leader was 'trying to turn the Tory party of one particular class into the Conservative Party of the nation'.

Eric Evans[3] has pointed to another feature of the *Tamworth Manifesto*. If it is better known for its attempt to convince popular opinion that the leadership was prepared to accept the spirit of the age and take up the cause of moderate reform, the document was nonetheless also designed to win support from many of Peel's opponents within the Conservative Party. Some were never likely to give him their backing but the more realistic among them knew that there was no obvious alternative leader and were prepared to accept any olive branch which he held out to them. The concession, in one of the few specifics of the Manifesto, was the promise of action to revive the fortunes of the Church of England by removing certain irritating and irrational abuses concerning the conditions and rewards of the clergy. This was important in a party which viewed the Church as one of the key English institutions, the more so as the emancipation of the Catholics a few years earlier had created doubts about the strength of Peel's commitment to Anglicanism. As Evans remarks: 'The landed Tories would neither love nor fully trust Peel. For the moment, however, they were happy to follow him'.

Although the manifesto was, in Gash's words,[4] 'an electioneering document on a grand and unprecedented scale' and acquired national coverage, it was not enough to bring about a fundamental change in party fortunes. The time was not yet ripe for the Conservatives and despite having begun to develop their organisation (see pages 56–7), they were defeated in the election. The party improved its position, but was well short of a majority having won only 279 of the 658 seats. After several parliamentary defeats Peel resigned in April 1835.

e) Opposition, 1835–41

Peel quickly adjusted to the new situation, and stuck to his chosen path. He had no intention of allowing the Conservatives to revert to old Tory attitudes of narrow self-interest because he knew that they needed broader support in the community. But neither was he attracted to the strategy of seeking to outbid the Whigs by adopting a policy of bold reform in an attempt to win the support of radical opinion. At a time when the working classes lacked the vote, and neither party was interested in giving it to them, there was no electoral advantage to be gained from such a ploy. The times were too turbulent to make a widening of the franchise a realistic possibility, and Peel had no wish to consider it. He had no desire to ally with radicals within his own party or those outside. As he put it: 'My opinion is decidedly against all manoeuvres, all coquetting with radicalism for the mere purpose of a temporary triumph over the government'.

For Peel there was a middle way. This involved accepting the forces of change in society and coming to terms with them. It was really a similar policy of cautious reform to that which had been employed by Lord Liverpool in the 1820s, but which had come to an end when the Duke of Wellington became Prime Minister in 1828. After 1835 it was this path of creating a consensus of moderate opinion which Peel chose to follow. In line with this policy he developed the concept of responsible, non-partisan opposition. Not for him the approach of the Whig leader, Tierney, a decade earlier, who had asserted that 'the task of the Opposition is to propose nothing, to oppose everything and to turn out the government'. Instead, Peel was prepared to support the Whig government whenever it behaved in what he believed to be a reasonable and just manner. He openly backed some of its reforms, even to the extent of saving the government from defeat.

The Right doubted the wisdom of Peel's approach, but it gave him more time to put the Conservative house in order and to convince the voters of his ability and capacity for leadership. Never before had there been such a responsible and well-prepared Opposition. The policy paid electoral dividends. Until 1867 general elections were held after the death of the monarch, and in 1837 the Conservatives further advanced their position in the election that followed William IV's death. They won a majority of the seats in England and Wales, but the Whigs were kept in power by the strength of their support in Scotland and Ireland.

Peel's political skills were particularly apparent in the so-called Bedchamber Crisis of 1839. Melbourne resigned, and Queen Victoria reluctantly asked Peel to become Prime Minister. He requested the appointment of some Conservative ladies to serve in her bedchamber, rather than have her surrounded by the wives of Whig grandees. When she refused, Peel declined to take office. He felt that her attitude showed a lack of confidence in his leadership, and he would not compromise even though some of his supporters were impatient for another taste of power. Melbourne returned, and his ministry drifted on, until in June 1841 Peel successfully put down a motion of 'No Confidence'. The government fell and in the general election which followed the Conservatives were victorious.

f) The 1841 Election

Peel won a decisive victory, gaining a majority of 76 seats. Radical attacks on vested interests had driven many landowners into the arms of the Conservatives. But above all, members of the landed interest warmed to the Conservative pledge to maintain the Corn Laws. Many Conservative candidates had adopted a highly protectionist position, despite the fact that Peel felt that trading policy was too complex an issue to be settled in an election campaign. Gains were made in every type of constituency and in all areas of the country, although it is clear that the Conservatives were strongest in the counties and in the small boroughs, rather than in the larger urban areas. Their greatest strength was in England, especially in the Midlands, and the south and east (outside of London). In Wales, Scotland, the north and south-west there was less of a swing away from the Whigs.

Many factors contributed to the Conservative success. The anti-reform stance of the Tories in 1831–2 had passed into memory, and there was some reaction against the Whigs who seemed to have been in office for a long time (11 years). Their handling of the national finances had been inept, and they were disunited. The Conservatives had responded to the growth of the electorate by developing their organisation around the country (see pages 56–7) and were in a position to maximise their support. However, that support owed much to the past performance of their leader, and was a striking indication of

	1832	1835	1837	1841
England (out of 471)	129	209	244	283
Scotland (out of 53)	10	15	20	22
Wales (out of 29)	13	17	18	19
Ireland (out of 105)	33	38	32	43
Total (out of 658)	185	279	314	367

Number of Conservatives returned in Elections during the 'Age of Peel'

the regard many people had of his statesmanlike behaviour. No other politician was held in such high esteem, and as one contemporary put it, 'All turns on the name of Sir Robert Peel'.

The improvement in Conservative fortunes had been continuous since 1832, when the party had been at the lowest point to which either of the two main parties fell in the nineteenth century. By 1841 they were in power. They had been much assisted by the unusual circumstance of three elections in the first nine years of the reformed parliament. This was the only time in the 35 years between the first two Reform Acts that a minority Opposition took office after a general-election victory, and it was to be the only one in which the Conservatives were on the winning side. There was much relief in the country and in political circles that a strong government could now be formed. In 1841 the way seemed open to a new era of Conservative ascendancy.

A Note on ... Peel's Reorganisation of the Conservative Party

The Conservatives were the first of the national parties to begin to organise. In the year of the Reform Act, the Carlton Club was established as the new party headquarters. By the end of the decade the party was being run on the basis of an alliance between the leader, the Chief Whip and the Principal Agent. There was never a complete division of labour but broadly the leader and the Chief Whip were responsible for parliamentary matters, and the Conservative Election Committee, including the Chief Whip and the Principal Agent, looked after affairs outside Westminster.

a) At Westminster

In 1832, there was a mood of fractious disarray within the Conservative Party, following its election debacle. Peel understood the need for better management of the House and wished to tighten up on matters of discipline. He recognised that in order to achieve this, he needed to establish a better rapport with the rank and file. He addressed gatherings of the whole parliamentary party to explain some plan or policy and to plead for better attendance. In addition, he occasionally met its leading members at his Drayton home to discuss tactics and ideas. By such approaches, he imparted a sense of direction to the Conservative Party, though relations with some backbenchers were continually under strain.

b) The Carlton Club

The Carlton Club was the link between the party leadership and local Conservative 'notables' in the country. It provided a social centre for party members in both houses and influential supporters in the provinces, as well as a home for party management and organisation. The Whips had offices there, and with the aid of the Principal Agent they kept in touch with the constituencies, collecting information, bringing candidates and constituencies together, and maintaining contact with local associations and agents.

F.R. Bonham was the Principal Agent during the time Sir Robert Peel led the party. He was highly competent and he served his leader well. The two men were personal friends, and Bonham frequently met Peel to keep him informed of party feeling. Bonham's talent in running campaigns was evident in the 1835 general election. Soon afterwards, at his suggestion, a small, permanent Election Committee was set up to ensure a more organised and professional direction of local activity. It supervised elections, helping in the raising of money and the selection of candidates, as well as collecting information on the registration of voters in the constituencies.

c) Outside Westminster

Both Whigs and Conservatives established Registration Societies after 1832 to see that potential voters were placed on the electoral list. Within these Registration Societies, activists became adept at ensuring that likely party supporters were on the voting roll, and that the names of likely opponents were removed. As such, they were more often agencies of corruption than well-organised and disciplined organisations. Yet they represented an early form of election machinery, and demonstrated the way in which voters could be organised and directed. Their activities were co-ordinated by the London headquarters at the Carlton Club, which took a close interest in the state of local registration and party strength. Peel saw the importance of the development and in 1837 urged his supporters to 'register, register, register'. The effort was successful. By 1841 Conservative organisation nationally and locally was impressively developed.

2 Peel's Second Administration, 1841–6

> **KEY ISSUE** Why was Peel's government more widely admired in the country at large than in the Conservative Party at Westminster?

a) The Cabinet and Peel's Predominance Within It

Peel's Cabinet was an exceptionally impressive one, containing as it did five past or future prime ministers (in order, Lord Ripon (previously Lord Goderich), the Duke of Wellington, Peel himself, Lord Stanley and Lord Aberdeen) as well as other colleagues from previous governments. Its general character was predictable, for Peel gave office to many of the experienced men who had assisted him when the Conservatives were in opposition. The talented younger men – notably Gladstone, Herbert and Cardwell – were for the moment compelled to take a back seat, although Gladstone as Vice-President of the Board of Trade was to be deeply involved in devising and implementing Peel's free trading proposals. There was no room in the government for the ambitious Benjamin Disraeli, who does not seem to have been seriously considered. As only a recent entrant to the House of Commons there was little reason why he should have been. After all, his early Commons performances had been unremarkable and he had done nothing to impress the party leadership. But Disraeli felt resentful about his omission and was not much comforted by the letter he received from Peel in answer to his request to serve. The Prime Minister 'did not contest' the 'qualifications and pretensions' of many of his supporters 'whose co-operation I should be proud to have', but pointed out how 'insufficient are the means at my disposal to meet the wishes that are conveyed to me'. This 'rebuff' was eventually to drive Disraeli into the ranks of the malcontents on the backbenches, and Peel was to pay a heavy price for the new parliamentarian's wounded pride.

Peel's own authority was unchallenged. He had an unrivalled national reputation and was indispensable to the fortunes of the Conservative Party. His intellectual pre-eminence and his strategic vision gave him a dominance over his colleagues and as Prime Minister he had a clear sense of purpose and relentlessly drove his colleagues in the direction in which he wished to go. Government had a coherence which had long been lacking and, from the beginnings the ministry, was clearly embarked upon a mainly constructive path. Peel's rather aloof manner did not invite discussion. He was rather autocratic, and exercised an unusual amount of day-to-day control over the entire administration. He was very well informed about all aspects of policy, and had a masterly grasp of detail. Colleagues recognised how conscientiously he carried out his duties and were mostly willing to accept the lead he gave them. As Sir James Graham, the Home Secretary, explained: 'We never had a minister who was so truly a first minister as he is. He makes himself felt in every department, and is really cognisant of the affairs of each'. Although his colleagues were an unusually able group of men, Peel wished to be fully informed about every aspect of policy. As far as he was concerned responsibility ultimately lay with him, and so he took on a burden of work which was quite exceptional. He even introduced his own budgets, and Gladstone noted that government was not so much conducted by the Cabinet, as by the heads of department in individual consultation with the Prime Minister. It was this personal control which led to the allegation that the ministry was no more than a 'Cabinet of Peel's dolls'. No Prime Minister has subsequently so dominated the process of administration, and the growth in the scope and complexity of modern government business make it impossible for it to happen again. However, it is a tribute to Peel's performance that, when Ramsay MacDonald became the first Labour Prime Minister in 1924, he was presented with a set of the Peel Papers as the best guide to the role of Premier.

b) Financial and Social Reform

On taking over, Peel wanted to do something to improve the lot of the 'labouring classes of society'. He was appalled by the hunger and misery around the country, which was particularly severe in some areas. Britain had become increasingly urbanised and industrialised. Associated with these two phenomena were a series of appalling social conditions in the towns and cities which led to popular discontent. Peel was concerned about the threat to public order that this situation posed. Graham shared Peel's worries and was determined that any lawlessness should be quickly tackled, whether it came from Irish agitators, from Chartists, or from elsewhere. Alarmed at the excesses of working-class agitators, he urged magistrates 'to act with vigour and without parley'. He was nervous about the possibility of mob rule and was anxious to see large public meetings suppressed.

Tory backbenchers had no reason to complain about any lack of resolution on the government's part when it was faced with matters of law and order. But the government went further than firmly maintaining public order. This repressive policy was combined with reforming measures to ease social distress, and Peel felt that improvements in the level of general prosperity were necessary. This is not the place for a detailed critique of the work of his reforming ministry, but its achievements merit some explanation and indicate some of the strengths and deficiencies of the Peelite approach to public affairs.

When Peel took office in 1841 the national finances were in an unsatisfactory state. Lacking ideas, the Whigs had allowed the situation to drift, and five years of regular annual deficits had culminated in a cumulative deficit of the then huge sum of £2m. Peel took personal responsibility for the direction of affairs. He wanted to expand the economy and he lost no time in changing the thrust of government policy. The effect of his innovatory budgets was to liberalise trade by removing or reducing a large number of customs duties. To make up for the immediate loss of revenue he boldly reintroduced Income Tax, a tax on income from land which previously had only been levied in wartime. He explained his decision in the Budget speech of 1842:

1 It is my duty to make an appeal to the possessors of property . . . I propose that the income of this country should bear a charge not exceeding 7d in the pound; for the purpose of not only supplying the deficiency in the revenue, but of enabling me to propose great commercial
5 reforms, which will afford a hope of reviving commerce, and, by diminishing the prices of the articles of consumption, and the cost of living, will compensate you for your present sacrifices.

Although he was not a doctrinaire Free Trader, he became convinced of the need for tariff reductions. He hoped that they would lower prices and expand consumption to create a new prosperity from which all classes in the community would benefit. This would strike at the root cause of social distress, and bring about a general improvement in the standard of living. Some of his backbenchers feared that the government's adoption of free trade in one area meant that sooner or later it would be applied agriculture; they feared that the survival of the Corn Laws would be short-lived.

Other measures were introduced to strengthen the financial system. The Bank Charter Act of 1844 brought about much tighter control over the banking system. It increased the power of the Bank of England over note-issue, and placed greater controls over private banks. By so doing it paved the way for the eventual supremacy of the Bank of England and the structure Peel created lasted well into the twentieth century. As Briggs has noted: 'Although effective central bank management and techniques took years to evolve, the Victorians could look back to Peel as the architect of a confident economic order'.

The thinking behind the Companies Act, also of 1844, was not dissimilar. It set out to remove irregularities which a parliamentary committee had identified in 1844: 'For years, the world [has] been at the mercy of anyone who chose to publish an advertisement, call himself a company, and receive money for assurances and annuities'. The Act sought to increase public and commercial confidence in the reliability of businesses, by insisting that they should be registered and produce annual accounts. Like the Bank Charter Act, the Companies Act was concerned to end what Peel regarded as 'reckless speculation' and to ensure that business and commerce were put on a sounder footing.

In the area of social reform, Peel did little and what was offered was mainly in response to public pressure or as a result of the campaigning of committed individuals. The Mines Act of 1842 forbade the employment of women and young children underground, after the revelations of a Royal Commission had shocked public opinion. Graham's Factory Act reduced the hours which could be worked by women and children under 13, and with its requirement for the fencing of machinery it was a useful advance. Yet in both cases, it was the work of the philanthropic Lord Ashley (later Lord Shaftesbury) which drew the matter to government attention and provided the impetus for improvement. Peel and Graham were sceptical about the value of direct measures of social reform, regarding them as at best palliatives, and at worst a serious limitation on the freedom of manufacturers to run their enterprises as efficiently as possible. They believed that it was not the state's role to produce legislation to tackle social discontent. It was more important to ensure that there was plenty of employment and cheap bread available. Their view was that only by improving the purchasing power of the masses could the condition of the people be transformed.

c) Ireland

In 1841 disorder in Ireland was growing and many Irishmen were agitating for a repeal of the Act of Union between Britain and Ireland. Daniel O'Connell, the hero of the struggle for Catholic Emancipation, led the moderate movement which urged the need for change, but his leadership of the Irish cause was being challenged by a new generation of nationalists who were discontented with his lack of revolutionary fervour. Many of the firebrands were to be found in the 'Young Ireland' movement which was prepared to resort to force to achieve its aims. When O'Connell began to address a series of mass meetings which clamoured for repeal, the strength of his movement could no longer be ignored. The government was under pressure from *The Times*, the Duke of Wellington, and Irish Protestant peers to act firmly by clamping down on all agitation. A vast meeting to be held in Clontarf was banned and O'Connell was arrested, convicted and imprisoned. He was discredited, and the government's more hard-line supporters were relieved.

Although he was a firm believer in law and order, Peel wished to be constructive, and much of his Irish policy showed a liberality of outlook which was rare at the time. He was one of the few Conservatives of the nineteenth century to have any understanding of Irish issues, and was convinced that: 'Mere force, however necessary the application of it, will do nothing as a permanent remedy for the social evils of that country'. His aim was to gain the sympathy of wealthy and intelligent Roman Catholics in support of the Union, so that men of property in both Britain and Ireland could work together, irrespective of religious differences. If he was to achieve this goal, the grievances of the Catholic population needed to be addressed, for Peel appreciated 'the necessity of disuniting, by the legitimate means of a just, kind and conciliatory policy, the Roman Catholic body, and thus breaking up a sullen and formidable confederacy against the British connection'.

In its more conciliatory phase, the government hoped to win approval by a series of initiatives. An attempt at franchise reform met with opposition on the Tory Right, and Peel's attempts at tackling the thorny issue of land tenure met with a similar fate. He had established a Commission into agrarian problems, particularly those concerning land law, and when Lord Devon's committee reported, Peel put forward a Bill to allow for limited compensation to those tenants who carried out improvements. However, he was unable to carry it through the Lords because of opposition from hard-line peers and Irish landowners, and the proposal was withdrawn.

Peel also wanted the Catholic population to be given the chance to take up official positions, and this required the development of more educational opportunities. He was particularly keen to promote opportunities for the joint education of Protestants and Catholics, for he wanted to break down barriers between the two religious communities. However, this non-sectarian approach aroused great controversy. Peel wanted to see three new Queen's Colleges established to educate Irishmen irrespective of their religious creed, a proposal which was opposed by both Anglicans, who thought it ungodly, and Catholics, who wanted nothing to do with them.

More controversially, he wished to develop Maynooth College, Dublin, a Catholic seminary. In April 1845, the government offered £30,000 for rebuilding, and wished to increase the annual grant, in a bid to appease the Catholic clergy. To his credit, Peel pressed ahead with the proposal even though it was unpopular on all sides. Catholics were unimpressed and many of his Protestant supporters in the Commons were deeply affronted. They felt that Peel was striking a blow against one of the foundations of their Tory philosophy, namely support for the Anglican cause. Party unity was seriously strained and 149 backbenchers voted against the measure. Hostile petitions flooded in to Downing Street, a National Club 'in support of the Protestant principles of the Constitution' was established as a breakaway from the Carlton Club, and Lord Ashley led a Protestant Association committed to the repeal of the Act. Peel's popularity within the Conservative party was at a low ebb.

As the controversy raged, the issue at the heart of it came to matter less than did the personal honour of the Prime Minister. For many Tories, Peel's behaviour revived old suspicions. One compared him to Judas Iscariot, and commented that 'as Sir Robert Peel betrayed the Protestant Church in 1829, so he is going to betray the Protestant Church in Ireland in 1845. I can have no confidence in a man who obtained office by fraud, and who dares to trample underfoot the best interests of the country'. *Punch* expressed something of their contempt in its refrain:

How wonderful is Peel
He changeth with the Time,
Turning and twisting like an eel
Ascending through the slime.

As well as placing further strain on party loyalty in general, the Maynooth question severed most of the remaining bonds between Peel and the Tory Right. For the moment his position was secure as there was no one in a position to mount a challenge. However, the Irish potato famine was an even more sensitive issue, and it was shortly to provide the supreme crisis in Peel's career.

d) The Corn Laws

In the 1841 election the almost clean sweep the Conservatives had made in the county constituencies had depended on the pledge to maintain the Corn Laws. However, agricultural protection was never a matter of absolute principle for the Conservative leader, and he was willing to consider modifications to the existing arrangements. In 1842 he revised the sliding scale of duties which had been adopted in 1828, and soon afterwards he concluded that the Corn Laws should be repealed when the time was right. In his considerations he was influenced by the propaganda of the Anti-Corn Law League which argued for free trade and stressed that the effect of the Laws was to keep the price of bread artificially high. As we have seen, he was worried about the threat to public order, especially as high food prices were a cause of distress in 1842, when there was widespread Chartist activity.

By 1845 agriculture was in a privileged position as the only area of economic activity still substantially protected by tariffs against competing imports. Having examined corn prices at home and abroad, Peel concluded that this protection, in the form of the Corn Laws, was not necessary to assist the agricultural interest. He felt that the landowners' prosperity depended on efficiency and a strong home market, rather than any artificial barriers to trade. Therefore, he concluded, they did not need the retention of the Corn Laws. He was also convinced that, if the Laws were removed and grain was made more cheaply available, lower bread prices would not encourage manufacturers to reduce workers' wage levels. Careful analysis had persuaded him that wages did not vary with the price of corn. For instance, wages were relatively high in 1843 when bread prices were untypically low.

However, Peel's motives were more political than economic, for he knew that the Corn Laws were a cause of resentment, and that their removal would help to guarantee stability and order. They were seen by many people as a symbol of an outmoded past in which the aristocracy had possessed great privilege, and the middle and working classes had been denied a share of power. They were a reminder of the dark days after 1815 when an unpopular government had seemed to be acting in the interests of its own supporters only. As one contemporary observed, 'the Corn Laws are considered a class monopoly, and are thus most detrimental to aristocratic and to the landed interest'.

Peel's private thoughts on the inevitability and desirability of repeal were shared with only a few very close colleagues. He realised that many Tories in the House of Commons had a different outlook. They firmly believed in the protection of corn, and were already suspicious about his commitment to their point of view. His own Chancellor, Goulburn, gave him a warning in 1845 that:

1   An abandonment of your former opinions now would, I think, prejudice your character as a public man ... In my opinion, the party of which you are the head is the only barrier which remains against the revolutionary effects of the Reform Bill. If it be broken in pieces by a destruction of
5   confidence in its leaders (and I cannot but think that an abandonment of the Corn Law would produce that result), I see nothing before us but class animosities and the ultimate triumph of unrestrained democracy.

Within Peel's Cabinet there were serious differences of opinion and at first only three ministers supported him. However, such was his authority and so relentless his power of argument, that he won over the bulk of the others to his viewpoint. In the words of Norman Gash,[5] 'the debate seemed to revolve for the most part around the time, mode, justification and responsibility of abandoning them [the Corn Laws]'.

In party terms, the Cabinet was not Peel's main problem. He was aware of the deep distrust of his intentions on the backbenches. He hoped that he would be able to let the current parliament run its course and then fight the next election on the issue of free trade in corn. In that way he would not be so vulnerable to the charge of betrayal of the agricultural interest. Everything depended on the harvest, and as Gladstone remarked, 'one bad harvest, or at all events two, would break up the Corn Laws with the party ... it is a law mainly dependent on the weather'. The summer of 1845 was wet, and potato blight spread to the British Isles from continental Europe. In parts of England this meant hunger: in parts of Ireland it led to widespread starvation. Peel believed that something had to be done, for the sake of the working classes in Britain as in Ireland. In itself, repeal would not do much for the Irish peasantry who could not afford to buy bread but it would help protect British labourers from high bread prices in times of scarcity. Peel seized the opportunity to announce the suspension of the Corn Laws and the impossibility of reintroducing them.

e) Opposition to Repeal

Peel's action was a challenge to the fundamental beliefs of many Conservatives. He was now seen as the arch-traitor who had again let the party's supporters down on a major issue. Disraeli, disappointed at his lack of advancement, now had an opportunity to exploit the revolt to further his own career. He taunted Peel mercilessly and articulated the bitterness of the agriculturalists who saw protection as vital to their interests. Lord George Bentinck was their spokesman, and his backing made it possible for Disraeli to gather in their support. Bentinck wielded the sledgehammer and Disraeli employed the more deadly rapier.

Until this controversy Bentinck had rarely spoken in the House of Commons. Politics had never been his consuming passion. He was more interested in breeding and racing horses, and was a well-known, if controversial, figure on the turf where he was involved in several rows and duels. His main claim to national fame had been in 1844 when he had been prominent in exposing a fraud surrounding the Derby. As a country landowner and heir to a vast estate, he represented the sort of dilettante approach to politics which Peel despised. Yet Bentinck was no Ultra. In earlier times he had been Private Secretary to Canning, had supported the Whigs over reform in 1830, and had been offered a position by Peel in his Second Administration. Unlike many on the Right he had actually backed Peel over the Maynooth Grant.

It was the proposal to repeal the Corn Laws which aroused him to fury. He had never been closely associated with Disraeli, but between them 'the Jockey and the Jew' mounted a formidable assault on the Peelite leadership. Bentinck had none of Disraeli's subtlety or flair. He was much more given to extravagant and even violent language, and in 1845–6 he turned his biting invective on the leader whom he thought had betrayed his party. He was no orator, but his contemptuous manner made him effective in a brutal sort of way. He represented the raw anger of the agricultural lobby against a man whom they regarded as dishonourable, even treacherous. He reckoned that in bygone days the reprisals for Peel's behaviour would have been severe – 'I believe the punishment in the good old days for offences of this kind used to be cropping the ears and putting the vagabonds in the pillory'.

Early on, Disraeli made the comparison of Protectionism in 1845 and the Protestant cause in 1828–9, and, after accusing him of tampering 'with the generous confidence of a great people and a great party', he went on to savage Peel at his most vulnerable point:

> Dissolve if you please the parliament you have betrayed and appeal to the people who, I believe, mistrust you. For me, there remains this at least the opportunity of expressing publicly my belief that a Conservative government is an organized hypocrisy.

Other Tory backbenchers expressed similar sentiments. They pointed to Peel's inconsistencies and his alleged lack of loyalty to party and principle. From Colonel Sibthorp, there was regret that 'the Treasury benches [were] so infested with the noxious animals called rats'.

Peel found much of the invective difficult to answer. He believed that he was acting rightly and consistently and in the interests of the whole community. Such was the situation that repeal was necessary, and as the queen's minister he must have the flexibility to act as he felt appropriate. If necessary he was prepared to disrupt his party in the struggle, and he was consoled by the belief that:

> If I fall, I shall have the satisfaction of reflecting that I do not fall because I have shown subservience to a party ... and preferred the interests of a party to the general right of the community.

f) Protectionism in the Conservative Party

Among the Conservative protectionists, there was much suspicion of the government's policies. There was also a personal element in their opposition. Bentinck had not forgiven Peel for failing to serve in Canning's government in 1827, and Disraeli felt that his talents as a parliamentarian had not been sufficiently recognised. Neither had ever found Peel personally congenial. Yet both had been supporters of his administration in the early years, and Disraeli only became very disillusioned as the lack of emphasis on traditional Tory values became apparent. Others in the Party were also increasingly uneasy at the Peelite approach to Conservatism, its tone and its direction. They thought that it placed too much emphasis on a moderate and consensual style, and too little on the old Tory principles. They watched Peel with growing anxiety and mistrust.

For many of them the repeal of the Corn Laws was the last straw. As landowners, they took it for granted that agriculture was at the heart of the country's prosperity. They thought that its protection from foreign competition was essential both to the nation and to the social and economic position of the aristocracy in the community. They believed that an abandonment of the Corn Laws would put their status and influence at risk, and they had no wish to see this imperilled at the behest of the manufacturers of the Anti-Corn Law League, who had been clamouring for repeal. The League felt that the Corn Laws symbolised the unjust predominance of agriculture over manufacturing, and that this was unacceptable. Many protectionists were determined to cling on to that privileged position, and particularly disliked the thought of a Conservative Prime Minister bowing to the pressure of the industrialists. The Corn Laws were seen by them as representing their last security against ruin, and they expected a Conservative government to retain them. It was assumed that the Party leader would defend, not undermine, the landed classes and their way of life. In this they were reflecting the unmistakable feeling of the whole agrarian community, for the campaigning of the farmers in 1845–6 was intensive. Tenant farmers as a group lacked direct representation in the House of Commons, but they lobbied the landowners who were there, both individually and via the local Protection Societies they had formed. They were determined that there should be 'No Surrender' over the Corn Laws. They urged Conservative MPs to defend the agricultural cause on the basis that the Party was the voice of the countryside. At first some landowners were hesitant about a challenge to Peel for they knew that the issue would be a divisive and damaging one, but their resolve was strengthened by this local pressure. The protectionists proceeded to act in parliament as a powerful 'third force', with their own unofficial leadership, organisation and national backing, and, as the Corn crisis unfolded, control of the Party gradually slipped out of Peel's grasp.

Although not all of the Conservative landowners opposed Peel, the bulk of them were hostile. In the final vote on repeal only 112 Conservatives supported him, while 241 voted against – the measure was only passed with Whig support. The scale of the revolt was greater than that over the Maynooth Grant, although the majority of those who opposed Peel then opposed him again in 1846. The strongest antagonism came from those MPs who represented rural areas, and even a few who were personally free traders joined with the protectionists in the parliamentary divisions. They bowed to the pressure of local feeling. Gash's research[6] indicates that 86 per cent of Conservative MPs representing the countryside rejected repeal, whilst of those who sat for larger boroughs only 54 per cent did so. Clearly, much depended on the type of constituency MPs represented.

g) Peel's Handling of the Issue

Following the passage of the act repealing the corn laws many of the landed gentry were furious at Peel and they helped to bring about the defeat of the government on a bill to strengthen its powers in dealing with violence in Ireland. Whigs and protectionists combined against him, and Peel resigned in June 1846. The Conservative Party was now fundamentally split between the minority group of young men who saw Peel as their guide and mentor, and the majority group of protectionists among whom Disraeli had acquired considerable standing.

For Peel, good government was at stake, and repeal, as he later told his Tamworth constituents, tended to fortify the established institutions of the country, to inspire confidence in the equity and benevolence of the legislature, and to discourage the desire for further reform in the constitution of the House of Commons. As such it was a highly conservative measure and, like the 1832 Reform Act, the removal of just that sort of grievance which, untackled, leads to revolution. He had a good case from the point of view of a far-sighted conservative who wanted to defend the conservative cause, but from the point of view of the Conservative Party and its major supporters the repeal was a devastating blow.

Robert Blake,[7] a leading authority on the Conservative Party, has claimed that Peel's decision was sound enough, but that in his handling of the issue he was maladroit: 'It was Peel's merit as a statesman that he normally adapted his policies to the need for change. It was his deficit as a politician that he did so in a manner which, combining as it did, prickliness, egotism, self-exculpation and unctuousness, gave a formidable handle to his enemies'.

Certainly, Peel's personality was an important factor in the break-up of the party. That schism was itself the culmination of a series of skirmishes between the leader and those whose support he needed to retain. By his actions, and the manner in which he went about them, he bears a responsibility for wrecking the party he had done so much to create. To Blake, it is, therefore, really from 1846 and not 1835 that modern Conservatism should be dated. For whilst Peel was in the wilderness, Disraeli and Bentinck lived to fight another day. The modern party emerged out of the confusion of the Corn Law conflict.

3 Assessment of Peel's Contribution to the Conservative Party

> **KEY ISSUES** What was Peel's legacy to the Conservative Party? How have different historians assessed his contribution to the party and country? Is it true that he was too ready to sacrifice the interests of his party to what he believed were those of the country?

In 1850, four years after his fall from office, Peel died as the result of a riding accident. For years his reputation had been almost unchallenged in the country, and he enjoyed immense popularity. On his death large numbers of workingmen sent in their pennies to pay for statues in his memory, and the scores of them erected in the industrial towns of the north reveal him to the nation as a Victorian hero – a fine example of the gospel of hard work. Tributes to his leadership of the country and the nation were paid by many writers and politicians. *The Manchester Guardian* noted the 'most striking and extraordinary expression of public feeling', but the *Times* obituary elaborated on Peel's contribution to national life, pointing out that he 'has been our chief guide from the confusions and darkness that hung around the beginning of the century to the comparatively quiet haven in which we are now embayed'.

That he dominated early-Victorian politics is a commonplace. He was at the centre of political life for approaching forty years and few would deny that during that period he proved that he was a highly capable statesman. He has had a good press both in his own time and subsequently. Bagehot was simultaneously drawn to and repelled by him, but acknowledged him to be a fitting man for his times, and above all 'a great administrator'. Disraeli observed that 'he was a transcendent administrator of public business and a matchless master of debate in a popular assembly'.

More recently, Lord (formerly R.A.) Butler,[8] a moderate (post-war) Conservative thinker and politician, saw himself as a follower of Peel. As a believer in practical reform, he admired Peel as an exponent of 'the art of the possible'. He admired his early work at the Home Office, where he demonstrated a firm approach, but combined this with a policy of reform. Of the later period, Butler felt that Peel had been in error over the 1832 Reform Act, but was impressed by the way in which he adjusted to its consequences and proceeded to 'build [our] modern creed'. He related that when he and his colleagues were attempting to restate Conservative principles after 1945 they used the Tamworth Manifesto as their starting-point.

A significant amount of the more academic writing about Peel has been contributed by Asa Briggs,[9] for whom his administrative pre-eminence, his industry and his sense of responsibility were praiseworthy qualities, as were the thoroughness of his grasp of detail and his capacity to take decisions. He believes that between 1841 and 1846 Peel's finest qualities were revealed; he 'impressed his personality and outlook on his well-balanced cabinet with exceptional force'. Donald Southgate[10] has written of Peel's 'moderation and empiricism', and of his skills as an administrator and parliamentarian. Donald Read[11] has portrayed him as 'the hero equally of the newly enfranchised, propertied middle classes and of the unenfranchised, propertyless masses', suggesting that for all of them he showed that the British political system 'under strong leadership, was capable of reacting purposefully to their needs'. But probably the historian who has written most prolifically on Peel has been Professor Norman Gash.[12] He has produced numerous articles and books from a sympathetic standpoint. These present a picture of Peel as the architect of the mid-Victorian era of stability and prosperity which, sadly, he did not live to see. In particular, Gash commends Peel's response to the issue of the Corn Laws, which 'did more than anything else to heal the social breach and restore the confidence in a political system that was still aristocratic and oligarchic'. He sees Peel as having exercised 'unrivalled leadership at the centre of power ... His place as the founder of modern conservatism is unchallengeable'.

Yet challenge has been made. In recent years, there has been a considerable amount of revisionist thinking applied to Peel's contribution to British politics in general and to the Conservative Party in particular. Boyd Hilton[13] has portrayed his approach as being dogmatic rather flexible, divisive rather than consensual. He rejects the idea that Peel handled each issue on its merits, adapting as the case demanded. Far from being concerned with 'the art of the possible', he was actually a man of an unswerving free market, capitalist vision who was prepared to thrust his views upon the country irrespective of whether they suited the matter under discussion.

Eric Evans[14] has also questioned the Gashite perspective in his valuable *Lancaster Pamphlet* which provides an effective synthesis of critical thinking about Peel. Evans own assessment of Peel's merits has undergone some change, as he readily admits. Whereas once he stressed Peel's 'extraordinary . . . ability' and was generous in his praise for the 1841–6 administration, his current position is less flattering. He draws attention to Peel's lack of creative talent and his record of opposition to changes such as parliamentary reform and the secret ballot, and his late conversion on issues such as the emancipation of Catholics. He highlights his poor relationship with his party, the way in which he despised some of the backbenchers who sat behind him in the House and the way in which between 1841 and 1845 [he] 'either ignored his followers' sensibilities or bludgeoned them into submission'. For good measure, he adds that Peel 'proved himself untrue to their Tory principles on Ireland, on religion, on commerce and, finally and fatally, on the English landed interest itself'. The picture suggests a politician who had serious deficiencies as a party leader.

A refreshing analysis has been provided by Bruce Coleman.[15] In his study of Conservatism, he has looked at the party from a more sceptical viewpoint. Stressing its defensive reaction to an often-threatening world, he sees its fundamental purposes being to prevent change and to defend the self-interest of the men of property. He is unconvinced by much of the analysis of Conservatism, for he detects that: 'The party's most familiar figures were being elevated not just to the Pantheon of the Good, but also to the Pantheon of the Progressive'. None of them were portrayed as solid Tories, but rather as Liberal Conservatives; Peel and Disraeli being 'the most conspicuous beneficiaries of this tendency'. He believes that many studies have been written by sympathetic historians who were keen to present a 'sanitised version', or by post-war writers who were personally liberal progressives and who wished to believe that such men as Peel and Disraeli were of a similar persuasion. By contrast, Coleman views Conservatives as people who wished to 'stem change, not to encourage it', and observes that many possessed an evident distaste for much of what the nineteenth century had brought them.

Such an approach stresses the essential cautiousness of Conservatism, and in Peel's case it is worth remembering that he suffered from a degree of nervousness about social disorder which was unusual even among Tory politicians. Twice, in 1831–2 and 1842, he sent ammunition down from London, and fortified Drayton Manor to defend it against rioters from the neighbouring industrial districts. His insistence that the government must move quickly to stabilise the constitution was clearly influenced by his fears for life, family and property.

Coleman's views are helpful in reminding us of the limitations of Peel's more enlightened Conservatism. The stern defender of Peterloo and the Six Acts was later a firm opponent of the extension of the franchise, and though Peel is often portrayed as the man who was willing to introduce necessary reform, it was often an acceptance of change he could not easily avoid. He opposed several constructive measures of the time until their passage became inevitable, 'his perception of necessary action came, almost invariably, at the eleventh hour'. Of his great achievements, most were significantly by way of 'repeal'. He knew how to clear the ground, but was not the man to build upon it. Most of the legislation he was responsible for derived not from his own thinking, but from the suggestions of others, and when he took them up they were a commonplace of social thought. The prospect of change was in many ways abhorrent to him, yet it is surely to his credit that when convinced of the need to act, he was willing to translate other people's ideas into concrete action. He knew when to give way, and did not shirk from the challenge, however unpopular it might be.

Coleman recognised that there was an element of fear in Peel's approach to reform. The experiences of 1828–32 seem to have convinced Peel that issues which jeopardised political and social order should be settled when the opportunity offered. 'Letting sleeping dogs lie' was too dangerous. Better to anticipate inevitable change, so that the terms of adjustment were controlled by the 'friends of order' rather than dictated to them by opponents. His reactions may have put strains on his supporters, but they shared his firm resistance to agitation and radicalism.

a) Peel and the Conservative Party

For some Conservatives, Peel is an unsatisfactory figure, and it is significant that references to him in party literature are often cursory and not wholly flattering. This is not altogether surprising for he gave a lower priority to party unity than any of his successors have dared to do. If he can be credited with the refashioning of the Conservative Party in the 1830s, so he must share some of the blame for its schism in 1846. He always placed much strain on the loyalty of his followers, and was unable or unwilling to woo them round to his viewpoint. Sometimes, his manner seemed to exacerbate their antagonism.

In a speech delivered in Tamworth to mark the 150th anniversary of the publication of the manifesto, Leon Brittan, a Home Secretary of the early-Thatcher era in the 1980s, reassessed Peel's work. Noting that the *Tamworth Manifesto* marked 'the beginnings of the modern Conservative Party', he contrasted the fortunes of Peel and Disraeli in party mythology. The one was solidly northern, solidly commercial and in spirit solidly middle-class, and 'lacked that elusive magic from which golden myths are spun'. By contrast, Disraeli had flair. His memory was perpetuated soon after his death by the formation of the Primrose League, and subsequently by countless Tories anxious to place themselves in the Tory tradition. Indeed, at the annual party conference, it is rare for no one to seek to invoke the Disraelian spirit. As Brittan notes: 'Conservative politicians daily jostle to claim some part of the legacy of Peel's great enemy and successor, that brilliant showman, Disraeli'. His words are quoted, re-quoted and frequently misquoted, 'but no primrose blooms for Peel'. Yet this was the man who towered over his contemporaries on the political stage, and Brittan stresses that the *Tamworth Manifesto* signalled a new Conservative attitude to reform. Indeed, he was keen to associate the Thatcher government of the 1980s with his policies, with its emphasis on economic liberalism to create prosperity, on an appeal to the solid middle class and on the blessings of the alleged 'trickle-down' effect to the mass of the population.

Of course, one reason for the downplaying of Peel in the party's history is that he placed less emphasis on the traditional Tory principles which he is often accused of betraying. For the partisan, anxious to see the purity of party principle preserved, Peel is a suspect figure. Those who adapt principles to the demands of the moment are open to such a charge, the more so if they were once among the most vociferous in defending them. Yet moderates such as Lord Butler, and many others in the modern party, would feel that his willingness to make concessions and his ability to recognise the best time to give way are good reasons to admire him.

In the early 1970s another Conservative leader and Prime Minister, Edward Heath, was to face similar difficulties with the Tory Right when he reversed a number of policies which he had espoused in the 1970 election. The charge used against him was that he was going in for 'U-turns'. Or was he realistically adapting and compromising, recognising the needs of the moment? To go on pursuing a theory which manifestly seems no longer applicable, is surely against the national interests.

Peel could be said to be the pioneer of the political U-turn. He faced the dilemma of many statesmen. Were the interests that the party served best protected by an implacable (inflexible) resistance to the forces of change, or by a policy of tactical concession to the inevitable? Should prudent Conservatives seek to confront agitation, or to placate it with a show of moderation and legislative activity? Peel's instincts were for prudent concession at a safe moment. On certain issues it might be wiser to concede in good time and gain the credit, rather than to suffer humiliation at a later date. He saw the inevitability of change before others in the party, and knew when to give way. He met with the entrenched opposition of many Conservatives, and his relations with the party were inevitably strained. Ultimately, he failed to convince enough of its supporters of the merits of his form of Conservatism, and many of them particularly disliked the way in which he was often yielding to precisely those forces which he had hitherto spent so much time resisting. The *Morning Post* spoke up for a whole spectrum of right-wing opinion in 1845, when it looked back on Peel's career and saw it as 'one of insanity or treachery'. The editorial continued in this way:

1 We regard him as the most loathsome of public men. His abilities (which are unquestionable) only add to his odiousness. He prostitutes to the meanest purposes the talents which God has given him ... That the Tories should ever again have anything to do with him, we can not
5 suppose.

b) Party versus Nation

For Disraeli, party loyalty was the prime consideration, and he scorned the policy of graduated concession which in his novel *Coningsby*, he derided as 'Tory men and Whig measures'. He believed that men should 'stand by the principles by which they rise, be they right or wrong'. His greatest eminence was to come in the very different electoral conditions after 1867, and in a sense his voice is nearer to that of the twentieth century: 'Above all, maintain the line of demarcation between parties, for it is only by maintaining the independence of party that you can maintain the integrity of public men, and the power and influence of Parliament itself'. His apologia for party looked to the future, whilst Peel's defence of his actions looked to the past.

On two great occasions Peel changed his mind and felt compelled to act. In 1829 and again in 1846 he believed that he was placing the well being of the nation before all lesser considerations. He still thought in terms of the traditional standards expected of a minister of the Crown – that he should do his best to ensure just, efficient and stable rule, and that the monarch's government was carried on. In this way he was not a party politician in the modern sense of the term, and he did not hesitate to put the claims of duty and conscience first.

In saying that he was placing the interests of the country before his party, he had a good case. It would have been a better one if he had taken more time and trouble to make his followers aware of the reasons for his change of mind. Furthermore, it is a difficulty of his position that he was once associated with one set of policies, and then took over those of his opponents. If leaders do this whenever the national situation appears to require a reversal, it is not surprising if they stand accused of opportunism. Followers support their party leaders on the basis of established expectations, and it must undermine confidence in the standards of public life if they find that those expectations have been abandoned even more so, if they are not fully in the picture as to why the change is considered necessary.

Many would see Peel as the creator of the modern Conservative Party, in that he moulded it into a national, pragmatic and unideological party above sectional interests, and based upon the Tamworth Manifesto. If his career had stopped in 1841, when back in office with a large majority, his reputation as a Conservative would stand high. He had steered the party through many difficult times and had made it stronger and more efficient than it had ever been before. The difficulty was that after 1841 he had less time to spend on the party, and his inevitable neglect meant that tensions which were always present widened throughout his second ministry. In the end, he helped to split the movement he had so laboriously built up.

c) Peel's Legacy to Nineteenth-Century Liberalism

Peel did carry with him into the wilderness the support of many of the 'officers' of the party, even if he lost that of many of the 'troops'. The pro-Peelite Conservatives gave him their loyalty and continued to follow him personally whilst he was alive. They were men of substance, among the most able administrators of the time, and Lord Rosebery later wrote that: 'To be a Peelite was a distinction in itself; it denoted statesmanship, industry and conscience'. Rosebery was himself a Liberal Prime Minister of the late-nineteenth century, and the impact of Peel on late-Victorian Liberalism was considerable. Leading figures such as Gladstone and Cardwell eventually moved into the Liberal camp, and coloured its outlook. The Gladstonian party was Peelite in its general approach, with its practical objectives of efficiency, sound administration, limited reform, free trade and a careful approach to government expenditure.

Boyd Hilton[16] has expounded the case that Peel had more to offer the Liberal than the Conservative Party. Questioning Gash's view that he was the 'founder of the modern Conservative Party', he sees him as 'the progenitor (father) of Gladstonian Liberalism'. He emphasises the extent to which Gladstone, in tackling policies ranging over public finance, free trade and Ireland, adopted a similar perspective to Peel. Furthermore, both men took the same view about the responsibility of political leaders to tackle issues courageously, in the light of what they felt had to be done. For them, governments must be prepared to act beyond the interests of any one class or party, and persuade the people at large that what they were doing was necessary and appropriate. As Boyd Hilton puts it, they must 'persuade the toiling masses that there was a moral energy at the centre of the state which was not indifferent to their fears and aspirations'.

d) A Supremely Useful Statesman?

By the late 1850s the world of Peel was only a memory, but he was the man who had worked to fashion a compromise between the system he inherited and the necessities of the new industrial society, and who had helped to efface the old Wellingtonian image of a class resolutely opposed to reform. In that sense, he forms an essential link between the world of the early-nineteenth century and the later period. In the shifting and changing times in which he lived, he was well suited to guide the Conservative Party and the country into a more peaceful era of contentment and stability. As one of Disraeli's own characters wrote in *Coningsby*: 'What is the use of lamenting the past. Peel is the man; suited to the times and all that; at least we must say so and try to believe so; we can't go back'.

References

1 H. Laski, 'Robert Peel' in [ed.] *Great Victorians* (Pelican, 1935)
2 N. Gash, *Politics in the Age of Peel* (Longman, 1983)
3 E. Evans, 'Sir Robert Peel: Statesmanship, Power and Party', *Lancaster Pamphlet* (Routledge, 1991)
4 N. Gash, *Politics in the Age of Peel*
5 *Ibid.*
6 *Ibid.*
7 R. Blake, *The Conservative Party from Peel to Major* (Heinemann, 1997)
8 R. Butler, *The Conservatives: A History from their Origins to 1965* (Allen and Unwin, 1977)
9 A. Briggs, in H. Van Thal, ed., *The Prime Ministers*, vol 1 (Allen and Unwin, 1974)
10 D. Southgate, *The Conservative Leadership 1832–1932* (Macmillan, 1974)
11 D. Read, *Peel and the Victorians* (Blackwell, 1987)
12 N. Gash, *Politics in the Age of Peel*
13 Boyd Hilton, 'Peel: a Reappraisal', *The Historical Journal* (1979)
14 E. Evans, 'Sir Robert Peel: Statesmanship, Power and Party', *Lancaster Pamphlet*
15 B. Coleman, *Conservatism and the Conservative Party in Nineteenth Century Britain* (Arnold, 1988)
16 Boyd Hilton, 'Peel: a Reappraisal', *The Historical Journal*

Summary
The Primacy of Peel, 1832–46

Opposition 1832–41

1832 Peel became Leader in
House of Commons

1834–5 PM
— *Tamworth Manifesto*

1835–41 Opposition
— New Conservatism
— Responsible Opposition
— Electoral improvement
1835 and 1837

1841 Victory in general election

Office 1841–6

1841 Peel PM

Financial Policy
— Free Trade
— Income Tax
— Ending Whig deficit
— Commercial legislation
— Mines Act
— Factory Act

Social Policy

1846 Repeal of Corn Laws

Tory split into Protectionists and
Peelites

Working on Chapter 3

Presumably, your work on Sir Robert Peel will be more extensive than just reading this chapter. From this chapter you are likely only to be gathering information and ideas on 'Peel and the Conservative Party'. Your first task is to build up a set of factual notes under this heading. You might find it useful to use three subheadings: 'The Creation of the New Conservative Party', 'In Government, 1841–6', and 'The Corn Law Crisis, 1845–6'. In each section of your notes concentrate on Peel's effect on his party. When you have completed these notes, draw up a two-column table under the heading 'Assessment'. Restrict yourself to points directly relevant to the issue of Peel's effect on the Conservative Party. The two columns could be headed 'plus' and 'minus'.

Answering structured and essay questions on Chapter 3

Very often, structured questions require you to show your knowledge and understanding of a topic or an issue. Normally they also demand that you exercise your judgment. Decide which of these activities you are mainly being asked to carry out in each part of the following question.

a) On what principles did Sir Robert Peel base his new Conservative Party?
b) What evidence of these is provided by Peel's actions in Parliament between 1834 and 1841?
c) How far was Peel successful in persuading Conservative MPs to follow these principles up to 1846?

Many essay questions about Sir Robert Peel require you to make an assessment of his overall impact on British politics. Before answering such a question it is important to reach decisions about the timescale you will cover. What timescale are you expected to write about in each of the following three questions?

1. Sir Robert Peel's influence was as great after his death as it was during his lifetime. Do you agree?
2. Peel's active contribution to party politics was greatest before he became Prime Minister for the second time. Discuss.
3. Why was Peel unable to carry his party with him throughout his second Ministry?

Source-based questions on Chapter 3

1. Peel and the Conservative Party in the 1830s

Read the extract from the *Tamworth Manifesto* on page 53 and answer the following questions:

a) What did Peel mean by an acceptance of the 'spirit' of the 1832 Reform Bill? (*3 marks*)

b) What does the language of the extract convey about Peel's attitude to reform? (*3 marks*)

c) What are the strengths and weaknesses of the *Tamworth Manifesto* as a guide to Conservative Party thinking in the 1830s? (*4 marks*)

d) Using your own knowledge and noting the general-election results cited on page 56 examine Peel's claim to be regarded as the founder of the Conservative Party. (*15 marks*)

2. Peel and the Young Disraeli

Read the poem from *Punch* on page 63 and the extracts from Goulborn, Disraeli and Peel on pages 64–6 and then answer the following questions:

a) How do you explain the savagery of *Punch's* attack on Peel in 1845? (*3 marks*)

b) What dangers did Goulborn see looming for Peel and for the Conservative party in 1845? (*3 marks*)

c) In what way does Disraeli's speech confirm the validity of Goulborn's fears? (*4 marks*)

d) In the light of these extracts and your own knowledge of Peel's career how far do you agree with the view that he was a great statesman but a poor party leader? (*15 marks*)

4 The Predominance of Disraeli, 1846–81

POINTS TO CONSIDER

Benjamin Disraeli was in many respects an outsider on the British political scene. He successfully used the issue of protection to inflict fatal damage on Peel's 'new Conservative party' and then spent several years trying to rebuild the organisation and revive its electoral fortunes. Eventually, he came to dominate his predominantly aristocratic party and led it to victory at the polls in 1874. His rise is a fascinating story. His impact on Conservatism, both then and subsequently, has been enormous.

In this chapter, you need to concentrate on the central role of Disraeli in the events of 1867 and on the work accomplished in his Second Ministry of 1874–80. This will place you in a position to understand the basis of his approach to Conservatism and to assess his contribution to the party's direction ever since his death. Ask yourself about his legacy to Conservatism and why the party was and remains proud of him as one of its greatest figures.

KEY DATES

1846	Repeal of Corn Law.
1846–67	Disraeli emerged as leading party figure and helped to modernise its image.
1867	Piloted passage of Second Reform Act.
1868	Brief First Ministry.
1872	Crystal Palace speech; set out three key aims of Conservative Party.
1874	Became Prime Minister for second time.
1874–80	Second Ministry.
1880	Defeat at the polls.
1881	Death.

1 Party Politics in the Years Between 1846 and 1867

> **KEY ISSUES** Why was the Conservative Party in such disarray in these years? What does his involvement in the passage of the Second Reform Act tell us about Disraeli's character and abilities?

After the repeal of the Corn Laws, there was a period of confusion and instability in British politics. Party ties continued, but the labels

THE RISING GENERATION—IN PARLIAMENT.

Peel. "WELL, MY LITTLE MAN, WHAT ARE YOU GOING TO DO THIS SESSION, EH?"

D——li (the Juvenile). "WHY—AW—AW—I'VE MADE ARRANGEMENTS—AW—TO SMASH—AW—EVERYBODY."

Post-1846 the Conservative Party was in a confused and divided state. By then, Disraeli and the Protectionists had forced Peel out of office and both men were left waiting on events.

did not mean very much, and the personalities of key individuals – Peel himself, Disraeli, Gladstone and Palmerston – were more significant. Over the next 20 years or so the fortunes of these men largely determined the fate of governments, which could never be sure of securing a majority because there was no strong direction and control. The discipline, which had been a characteristic of Conservative voting in the period 1835–45, largely disappeared.

The issue which did much to bring about the state of party confusion and which had such a disastrous impact upon Conservative fortunes was, of course, protection. The Party was effectively out of power for a generation. Conservative governments took office on three occasions under the leadership of Lord Derby – in 1852, 1858–9 and 1866–8. But on each occasion they were in a minority position, and the years 1846–65 were ones when Whig-Liberal politicians were in the ascendancy.

Peel's abandonment of the Corn Laws created a situation in which there were two groups of Conservatives at Westminster – the Protectionists and the Peelites. He had decided that Repeal was the duty of the government but he had done little to prepare the party to support a measure which he had previously opposed. Repeal offended his party's natural inclinations as well as threatening to damage the pockets of many of its supporters. He had expected them to follow him, but many Conservatives shared Disraeli's view that parties stood for certain broad principles and policies, and that the ones to which the Conservatives laid a special claim were the Church and the landed interest.

a) The Peelites

As long as Sir Robert Peel lived, he was the undisputed leader of those who had supported him in 1846. He never resigned the leadership, but was unwilling to give any sort of lead. Neither did he make any attempt to reunite the party whose fortunes he had done so much to restore back in the 1830s. Both before and immediately after his death in 1850, the Peelites gave broad support to the Whig government of Lord John Russell. They called themselves Conservatives but they shared with the Whigs a commitment to free trade.

Peel's influence lived on for many years via the group of influential supporters with which he had surrounded himself. Chief among these was his arch-disciple, Gladstone, who was both puzzled and disappointed by Peel's stance after 1846. He could not understand how his old leader could let the Conservative Party collapse, and in effect say 'it has fallen, there let it lie'. He and others were in a difficult position, in which it was tempting for them to revert to old allegiances. After all, they were Conservatives by choice and by tradition, and had a deep attachment to the party. Some did hanker after a reunion with their former comrades, but most could not bring themselves to contemplate it. They deeply distrusted Disraeli, none more so than Gladstone, who could never forgive the cruel vindictiveness of his earlier attacks on Peel. They remained faithful to their dead hero's memory, especially in their devotion to free trade and financial economy.

For some time, the Peelites (or Liberal Conservatives as some called themselves) remained a separate group, declining in power and influence as time passed. Having 'no organisation, no whipper-in', they were, in Gladstone's words, 'a public nuisance'. They had a foot in both parties, but they belonged to neither. Gradually, however, the more prominent among them joined with the Liberal Party and came to invigorate it with their beliefs and with their intellectual prowess.

b) The Protectionists

After the break-up in 1846, the Protectionist group largely consisted of back-bench country gentlemen, with Bentinck and Disraeli there to rally them. Most of the brains and much of the talent of the Conservative Party had sided with Peel, which lends substance to the description which the Radical, John Stuart Mill, used when he called the Conservatives the 'stupid party'. Whatever their intellectual shortcomings, they clearly were the country party defending the interests of agriculture, which were also their own interests.

The Protectionists had a solid corps of support at Westminster but this did not provide the foundations for a wider party of popular feeling, for outside the ranks of the farming community no one wanted protection. It had not been difficult for Disraeli to exploit the self-interest of the gentry and rally them for a fight against repeal. It was harder to get the party back on its feet again, the more so as even Disraeli recognised that protection had run its useful course, and was no longer a politically viable policy. However, in seeking to shed the commitment to protection, Disraeli was asking his supporters to go against those instincts which he had encouraged them to express. The attempt inevitably aroused suspicions about his character and motives, for some members of the landed class felt that they had been used to further Disraeli's own career interests. Nevertheless, despite the risks, by 1852 he was saying to an old friend that protection was 'not only dead, but damned'. He hoped that his change of mind would help to win Gladstone, Graham, Cardwell and others back into the Conservative fold, but, like some of his own supporters, they were unconvinced about his sincerity and could not trust him.

c) Conservative Attitudes and Policies after 1846

After 1846 Protectionists and Peelites sat on the same Front Bench, Disraeli only three seats away from Peel. However, the future of the Conservative cause now lay with the Protectionists, led at first by

Bentinck and Disraeli. Their leadership was soon faced with an embarrassment when a practising Jew was elected for the City of London. Jews were not allowed in the House of Commons but both Protectionist leaders believed that they should be. Disraeli flung himself into the battle for Jewish admission when a bill was presented to parliament, arguing that Jews should be admitted as equals in a Christian country 'because they can show so near an affinity to you. Where is your Christianity if you do not let in their Judaism?'

Many of the squires on the Conservative back benches were less than convinced. For them Jewish birth and Tory politics were not easy bedfellows. The stand taken by Bentinck and Disraeli was generally unsupported in the party, and there was much criticism from the rank and file. This led to Bentinck's resignation, and opened up the question of the succession. Disraeli had obvious flair, but at this stage did not have much experience and there were doubts about his trustworthiness. But there was no one else who was nearly as effective as a parliamentary performer. There were few able rivals: most were too old, too inexperienced or too lacking in basic competence. Therefore, almost by default, Disraeli became leader of the Conservative Party in the House of Commons in January 1849. Lord Stanley led the party in the Lords and was its senior figure.

d) Lord Derby (Lord Stanley until 1851)

When Lord Stanley was offered the leadership of the Protectionists he faced a daunting task, for many of the ablest politicians were in the Peelite ranks. Few of the country squires were capable or valued spokesman. Indeed, many had rarely spoken before the Corn Law controversy – not for nothing did the contemporary political commentator Walter Bagehot see the Tory gentry as 'the finest brute-vote in creation'. Few backbenchers were of cabinet potential and there were even doubts about Stanley's qualifications. Many Conservatives commented on his 'cynical insincerity' and found him to be a none-too-scrupulous grandee. He was light-hearted and did not take his task too seriously, being more interested in horses. He was at home on the turf, and was a steward of the Jockey Club.

Derby was content to coast along. As his son told Disraeli, 'the Captain does not care for office, but wishes to keep things as they are and impede "progress"'. By contrast, Disraeli was hungry for office and this required a strengthened Conservative Party. For a while he was frustrated because in 1851 his leader failed to form a government because he did not have enough talent available. Stanley knew he was scraping the bottom of the barrel, and exclaimed 'Pshaw! These are not names I can put before the Queen'. Disraeli was both furious and depressed, for the cup of office had been dashed from his lips, and it was this experience which made him realise that Protection must be 'unequivocally removed'.

LORD STANLEY/DERBY (1799–1869)

-Profile-

1822	Became a Whig MP
1830	Joined Grey (Whig) administration; supported parliamentary reform
1833	As Colonial Secretary, responsible for abolition of slavery in British Empire
1834	Left Whigs over Irish policy
1841–5	Served in Peel's government
1845–6	Strong supporter of protection; opposed repeal of Corn Laws
	Became Conservative leader
1851	Succeeded to title 14th Earl of Derby
1852	Led short-lived, minority government
1858–9	.. ..
1866–8	.. ..

Enjoyed his social life; never wished to be a full-time politician.

Contributed little to the intellectual development of Conservatism; no party philosopher.

Derby on Derby

[I am] devoted to whist, billiards, racing, [and] betting.

Disraeli on Derby

There are a thousand things which ought to be done ... and which I am obliged to decline doing or to do at great sacrifice. As for our Chief, we never see him.

In 1852 the chance came again, and this time Lord Derby formed his first government. Most of the ministers were unknown and/or inexperienced, and when Disraeli admitted he had 'no knowledge of the subject-matter of his position' (as Chancellor), he was reassured by the Prime Minister that this did not matter, for 'they give you the figures'. Disraeli produced his Budget proposals, but they were defeated in the House of Commons in December 1852, and Derby immediately resigned.

In 1858 Derby again became Prime Minister at the head of a minority government. This time some of the dead wood in the last ministry had been removed and there were some new and more able recruits. Disraeli, again the Chancellor, was very keen to see a revival of Conservative fortunes and was searching for a strategy which might bring about success. He tried to persuade Derby to seize the initiative on an extension of the franchise, pointing out that 'our party is now a corpse, but it appears to me that, in the present perplexed state of affairs, a Conservative public pledge to parliamentary reform, a bold and decided course, might not only put us on our legs, but greatly help the country'. However, the practical difficulties of producing an agreed scheme were enormous and the bill which Disraeli drew up was insufficiently appealing to gain necessary parliamentary support from the Opposition. The government was defeated in a Commons vote and went out of office after the subsequent election.

Nonetheless, although he failed on this occasion to keep the Conservatives in power, by 1860 Disraeli felt able to take credit for his achievement in 'educating his party' and making it look ready for government. He claimed:

1 I found the Tory Party in the House of Commons, when I acceded to
   its chief management, in a state of great depression and disorganisation
   ... I withdrew the ... party gradually from the hopeless question of protection, rallied all those members who were connected either person-
5 ally or by their constituencies with the land, and finally brought the state
   of parties in the House of Commons nearly to a tie.

Seven years later Derby was back again in Downing Street to lead another minority government with Disraeli as leader in the House of Commons. This time the events leading up to the formation of the ministry were very different. Palmerston was dead, and Gladstone had taken up the cause of parliamentary reform. With Prime Minister Russell also in favour, Gladstone had put forward the government's proposals but they had been seen as too mild for most Radicals and too radical for most Whigs. The government was defeated in the House of Commons in 1866 by a combination of Conservatives and dissident Whig-Liberals. Russell resigned and the Conservatives returned.

e) Parliamentary Reform, 1867

It was important for the Conservatives to show that this time they could stay in power sufficiently long to establish that they were a party of government. If they could rally their own supporters and by their proposals divide the Liberals, then there was a chance that this might happen. The time was ripe for another attempt at enacting a measure of parliamentary reform.

Disraeli seized the initiative with a bold stroke of political opportunism. He was a master of the political arts and welcomed his chance to produce a measure which would identify the Conservatives as a party of reform and ensure the ministry's survival. He needed to act quickly because he wished to exploit existing Liberal disagreements over the franchise question in order to establish his own ascendancy in the party. Lord Derby's health was failing and if Disraeli could come up with a political success it might stand him in good stead when the leadership of the Conservatives became vacant.

The actual passage of the bill and Disraeli's twists and turns do not matter here, although they do illustrate his parliamentary skills.

Suffice it to say that his performance was widely recognised as a *tour de force*, for he manoeuvred adroitly to attract backing from any possible section of the House, even accepting amendments whose implications he did not fully comprehend.

By the time the Derby-Disraeli proposals had been discussed in the House of Commons they were far more radical than had been intended. Some sections had been lifted directly from Gladstone's Bill, while others had been taken on board along the way. Above all, the Conservatives had put an act on the statute book, and its effects on British political life were to be enormous. Although the redistribution of seats from the less populous to the industrial areas was modest, and nothing was done to tackle corruption, the right to vote was extended considerably. In the counties the electorate went up by nearly 50 per cent but it was in the industrial boroughs where the changes were more sweeping, and where the effects were to be so dramatic. The skilled manual workers were to be enfranchised, for the measure gave the vote to all householders who paid rates and lodgers who paid £10 a year in rent. In Leeds, for example, the number of electors rose from 8,500 to 35,000.

Even Derby described the measure as a 'leap in the dark' and a 'giant experiment'. Some suspected that Disraeli had deceived them and for others there was great anxiety. To Lord Carnarvon, personally a critic, the result constituted 'a revolution. The Conservative Party is in imminent danger of going to pieces now, if indeed it does not disappear in the deluge that the government are bringing on'. Like Cranborne, the future Lord Salisbury, who also feared the growth of democracy, he resigned from the government.

Disraeli had privately indicated to Bright that 'the working-class question was the real question', and that was the thing that demanded to be settled in a far more radical way than Disraeli originally intended. As a result of his actions, the whole balance of power in British politics had been shifted. For the result was that the working classes constituted a majority of voters in the boroughs, which in turn now made up a majority of the constituencies.

Disraeli had said of Peel that 'he caught the Whigs out bathing and made off with their clothes'. His backbenchers thought that he had now done the same, and whilst many admired his tactical skill others felt bamboozled and deceived. However, the Act was artfully designed to minimise the novel situation of an enlarged electorate. The fact that the franchise in the towns was tied to a property qualification, that many small boroughs had been placed within Conservative county seats and that the South and West remained so over-represented made sceptics realise that all was not lost, and that there was some hope of 'taming the new democracy'.

The clash in 1867 was one of the first major parliamentary battles between Gladstone and Disraeli who were to be such formidable adversaries in the years ahead. Gladstone concentrated on the precise details, and attempted to expose the Bill's inadequacies. Disraeli managed to isolate him and to establish a temporary Tory-Radical alliance. For the moment Disraeli seemed to have the advantage. Derby had not been well for some time, and in February 1868 he resigned. On his advice the Queen sent for Disraeli as the new Prime Minister. At a party thrown in his honour he agreed that: 'Yes, I have climbed to the top of the greasy pole'. Bright, who had watched his performance in the House over several years, observed that this was 'a great triumph of intelligence and patience', the more remarkable in a 'party full of prejudices and wanting in brains'.

2 Disraeli, His Background and Early Career

> **KEY ISSUE** How is it that, in spite of his seeming disadvantages, Disraeli managed to emerge in these years as a leading Conservative?

Benjamin Disraeli was born in 1804 the grandson of a Jewish immigrant who had changed the family name from D'Israeli into its more acceptable Anglicised form. His father had sent the young boy to local private schools and had had him baptised into the Christian faith, as an Anglican. The young Benjamin began his working career as a writer. His first novel, *Vivian Grey*, was published in 1826. His hero was, in his own words, 'an elegant lively lad with just enough of dandyism to preserve him from committing gaucheries, and with the devil of a tongue'. The description might well have fitted Disraeli himself.

It was not easy to take the young Disraeli seriously for he was reckless in his personal life. He was a gambler – constantly in debt – who had chosen an unconventional and reckless life-style and had had several relationships with married women. He remarked that 'my nature demands that my life should be perpetual love', and he did much to ensure that this requirement was met. But when he met Mrs Wyndham Lewis, 12 years his senior, his life was changed. She immediately impressed him, for she was in his eyes 'a pretty little woman, a flirt and a rattle [chatterbox]; indeed, gifted with volubility I should think unequalled'. She told him that she liked 'silent, melancholy men', of which he was a prime example. In 1837 she persuaded her husband to allow Disraeli the use of the family rotten borough of Maidstone as a way of entering the House of Commons, and when she became widowed two years later the two of them married. Marriage provided Disraeli with enough money to clear his accumulated debts. In addition, his new wife gave him support and took his aspirations seriously: 'she believed in me, when men despised me'.

In the 1830s Disraeli had made five unsuccessful attempts to enter the House of Commons, firstly as a Radical, then as an Independent, and finally as a Conservative. Maidstone was the solution to his difficulties and he joined the ranks of the backbenchers who supported Sir Robert Peel. The Maiden Speech which he made was a fiasco. As always he was extravagantly dressed, bedecked with bangles and jewels, and reeking of exotic perfume. It was not surprising that MPs did not take his remarks seriously. Although his speech was carefully prepared, its numerous classical allusions and convoluted style were not well attuned to the audience, so that by the end he was being hooted down in derision. This provoked his famous reply: 'I sit down now, but the time will come when you will hear me!'

Fortunately, he was well advised by an Irish MP to 'get rid of your genius' for a while, 'speak often ... be very quiet, try to be dull ... astonish them by speaking on subjects of detail. Quote figures, dates, calculations, and in a short time the House will sigh for the wit and eloquence which they all know are in you'. Less flashy dress and demeanour also helped him along, and soon he did acquire a reputation as a lively speaker and a spirited debater.

At first he was a loyal supporter of Peel, 'the only hope of England'. Although he was disillusioned by his failure to gain office in 1841, he generally voted for Peelite measures until 1843. Then he began to develop distrust for the Prime Minister's approach, seeing him as insufficiently strong in his convictions. At first, he criticised his Conservatism rather than the man himself, and denounced 'Tory men and Whig measures'. But then the attack was widened. He teamed up with some young aristocrats who had entered the House in 1841 and they collectively referred to themselves as the 'Young England' group. George Smythe and Lord John Manners were leading members. They and others became the basis for characters in *Coningsby*, Disraeli's novel which was published in 1844, and in which the *Tamworth Manifesto* was attacked as an 'attempt to construct a party without principles'. They all shared a similar desire to return to earlier days before the dawn of industrialisation, times when landed Tories ruled the nation. In the words of Manners:

> Let wealth and commerce, laws and learning die
> But leave us still our old nobility.

Young England members came to despise the consensus politics of the Peelite party, so influenced by the new forces of industry and commerce. They hankered for a return to the days when the aristocracy possessed a paternalistic role as defenders of the mass of people from the evils of industrial life. They strongly disliked the New Poor Law of 1834, with its hated 'bastilles', and showed some sympathy for the Chartists, whilst not approving of any extreme behaviour. They were, in Blake's words,[1] 'swimming against the tide, but it was not an ignoble effort to want to see a return to a less harsh world'.

The group faded away after its members divided over the right approach to adopt over the Maynooth Grant in 1845 (see pages 62–3), and they were similarly divided over the Repeal of the Corn

Laws. On both issues Disraeli was on the opposite side to Peel, representing the Ultras rather than the new Conservatism which was so much more appealing to middle-class men of business. By his oratory and, in particular, the scathing attacks on Peel and his creed, he was damaging not only the Prime Minister but also the party. If Peel might have handled the Corn Laws with more tactical skill and concern for people's feelings, it was nonetheless Disraeli who so effectively 'put the boot in' and by his actions helped to put the party out of office for a generation.

After the splitting up of the Conservative Party, Disraeli controlled the fortunes of the anti-Peelite forces, even if the formal leadership lay in the hands of Bentinck and Stanley. They had the titles and connections, and were more obvious leaders of a primarily landed party. But Disraeli had the flair which was so much needed, and well before he reached the top, his ability was widely conceded. *The Times* commented on his contribution in 1860:

1 Let the Conservative Party never forget the hopeless state in which
   they were when fortune sent them Mr Disraeli for a leader. They had
   grown weary of a chief who was too liberal for their views of national
   policy, and avenged themselves upon him by an act of renunciation
5 which left them without leaders. They were irretrievably committed to
   an unpopular cause. Gradually, Mr Disraeli has weaned his party from
   their most flagrant errors. He has taught them to profess a sympathy
   for the great body of their countrymen and to recognise the necessity
   of looking to public opinion for support. When he found the Tory
10 Party, they were armed in impenetrable prejudice; under him, they have
   become competitors with the Liberals in the career of progress.

Not so much in the pursuit of this 'progress', but more with the aim of making his party credible and fit for a prolonged spell in office, he 'dished the Whigs' in 1867 over parliamentary reform. After this he was the obvious contender for the vacant leadership when Derby retired from the scene. Until then, he was by his own description 'the educator of his party', the man who had done so much to wean it from old attitudes and make it come to terms with the current situation.

a) How and Why Disraeli got to the Top

Disraeli's rise 'to the top of the greasy pole' was a remarkable and in some ways surprising achievement. He possessed many seeming disadvantages which he was fond of recalling in later life. Victorian England was a status-ridden society, and governments were garrisoned by gentlemen of great wealth. He appeared to lack most of the obvious qualifications for leadership of a party which numbered so many titled names amongst its members.

As he portrayed his past, he had been a nobody, he came from a poor background, and had not attended a famous school or university. The lack of a conventional public school or higher education was certainly unusual in the nineteenth century, he and the Duke of Wellington being the only prime ministers not to attend university. More seriously, he was a Jew, and every habit and tradition of the age made this seem an insuperable barrier to surmount. He had been compelled 'to struggle against a storm of political hate and malice which few men ever experienced'. Of course, to some extent this was a result of his own wounding speeches and the distrust which his behaviour inspired. The omens did not look good.

These disadvantages have often been exaggerated. His father was educated, cultured, comfortably off and well established in literary and professional circles. His marriage eased his financial problems and helped to put his 'doubtful' early reputation behind him. He certainly lacked rank but he was able to buy himself into the landowning fraternity by purchasing a manor house at Hughenden in 1848. This gave him property, even though he never lived the usual life of a country gentleman, and he neither shot nor hunted. Similarly, baptism into Christianity gave him religious respectability. However, his obvious Jewishness was still a barrier at a time when anti-semitism was rife. At the end of his disastrous maiden speech in the House of Commons, there had been derisive references to 'Shylock', which was how *Punch* portrayed him. Lord Cranborne, later to be his successor as Conservative leader, dismissed him as a 'Jewish adventurer'.

Even allowing for the fact that the barriers he had to overcome were exaggerated, it was no mean achievement for Disraeli to reach the top. His was not a promising background, it was a steep ladder to climb and there is no doubt that in ascending it he came up against the hostility and prejudices of many in his party. That he was successful was partly a matter of ability. He was a superb parliamentarian – skilful and courageous, and a master of the inimitable turn of phrase. He was often opposed by many great performers in the House of Commons, but he invariably countered their oratory with resourcefulness, ingenuity and his own particular eloquence. His speaking and debating talent was recognised by Derby, who acknowledged the ability even if he doubted the honour of his colleague. Lord Malmesbury, a future Foreign Secretary, also observed it and, on Bentinck's resignation, he remarked that, 'no one but Disraeli can fill his place ... it will leave [him] without a rival, and enable him to show the great genius he undoubtedly possesses'.

The observation points to another key fact, the absence of any real competition. Bentinck had remarked that Disraeli was 'the only man who came up to his ideas as an orator'. The longer the party had remained in the wilderness, the more it was apparent that there was no one else of remotely comparable quality. He was still not liked by many Conservatives and was seen as an outsider but, despite his lack of rank and his alien race, he established an obvious ascendancy over those around him.

Once so colourful, sparkling and extravagant, the Disraeli of later years
showed signs of being careworn. His course facial features in this portrayal
suggest a hint of melancholy, perhaps depression (see the description on
page 104). He seems very elderly for a man of 65 and within a few years was
to remark that power 'has come too late'.

Beyond these considerations, there was one other factor, his own relentless search for fame and power. It was, as Machin[2] puts it, a 'compelling pursuit. He would not be content with an obscure or subordinate role, but was always trying to urge himself to the front'. In this, he was like his hero in his first and semi-autobiographical novel. As Vivian Grey put it: 'Power! Oh! what sleepless nights, what days of hot anxiety! what exertions of mind and body! what travel! what hatred! what fierce encounters! what dangers of all possible kinds, would I not endure with a joyous spirit to gain it!'. For thirty years, Disraeli was intent on achieving such power, and he acted as pragmatically as the circumstances demanded, discarding any policies which appeared to be a barrier to his ambitions.

b) Disraeli's Character

Disraeli was one of the most colourful personalities of the nineteenth century. He had abundant charm, and women found him particularly attractive. His conversation was witty and sparkling, and he was a romantic, with a past reputation as a *roué.* The hint of disrepute made him all the more interesting, and his pleasing manner, with its lack of pomposity, was enough to beguile many. He was also an arch-flatterer who told women, in particular, what they were pleased to hear. The Queen was susceptible to his engaging personality and appreciated his flattery, and he saw that, when dealing with royalty, it should be laid on 'with a trowel'. He adored female company and was more at ease within it. Surrounded by men he could feel lonely and awkward.

His wife doted on him and he was devoted to her. It was a marriage which remained fresh and young, and he told her that she was 'more of a mistress to him than a wife'. From his early days his easy relationship with women gave him an entrée into the fringes of London society, and once he had a foot in the door he was able to impress people with his charm and wit. He had a great desire to make a name for himself and win renown so that he could make a lasting impression in his chosen career as a writer and politician. Yet, as Machin[3] points out,

1   although he knew the world intimately and lived very much in it – constantly attending dinner parties and making visits as a guest to country houses – he was never entirely of it. He reserved a separate personal area of retreat, from which he contemplated in ironic literary detach-
5   ment the doings and foibles of his fellows ... Even when he occupied positions at the very centre of power, he remained an outsider with a strong exotic touch. The sense of mystery which attended him, oddly combined with his willingness (especially as he grew older) to accept all conventional norms, added considerably to his effectiveness ... he [con-
10   tinued] to excite widespread curiosity by his individuality. If Gladstone was 'the People's William', Dizzy was the people's Asian wonder.

Whereas in his younger days he was often described as 'adventurous' and 'imaginative', among the more flattering epithets, by his twilight times he had so gained in popular appeal that he acquired a new dignity and air of authority. His earlier rakishness and disreputableness had been absorbed into a different image in which he was still exotic but was also a figure of drama, romance and mystery. His death left Westminster a duller place. By then, parliament had come to respect him. Until his last days, when his concentration and energy were undermined by ill health, his performance always commanded attention.

c) Disraeli as Prime Minister, 1868, and in Opposition, 1868–74

Disraeli's ministry was a short one for his government was still in a parliamentary minority. He called for a dissolution as soon as the new electoral registers were ready. The new electorate did not reward him, for as J.S. Mill remarked, it said 'thank you, Mr Gladstone'. The Conservatives were soundly beaten and Gladstone became Prime Minister.

Out of office, Disraeli soon successfully resumed his career as a novelist. Generally he was content to sit back and allow his arch enemy to make mistakes, and there was some dissatisfaction within the Party at his lack of positive leadership. Attempts were made to replace him with the Earl of Derby, son of the old Prime Minister, but he withstood the challenge and his political fortunes began to improve as the Liberals ran into difficulties.

Disraeli had deliberately opted for low-key opposition while he took steps to put the party organisation into better shape. However, by 1872 he felt ready to launch his offensive against the government. In a speech given at Manchester, for which he fortified himself with two bottles of brandy which he slipped into his water-jug, he mocked the Liberal Front Bench:

1   As I sat opposite the Treasury bench, the Ministers reminded me of one of those marine landscapes not very unusual on the coasts of South America. You behold a range of exhausted volcanoes. Not a flame flickers on a single pallid crest. But the situation is still dangerous. There are
5   occasional earthquakes, and ever and anon the dark rumbling of the sea.

He also pointed to Gladstone's preoccupation with political reform, at the expense of social improvement, and stressed that 'the first consideration of a minister should be the health of the people'. He coined the phrase '*sanitas sanitatum, onmia sanitas*', a parody of a Biblical allusion, which loses something in translation – 'health of health, all is health'. He condemned the Liberals for their irreverent attitude to established institutions, and stressed Conservative loyalty to the monarchy, the House of Lords and the Church of England. He also denounced the government's supine attitude in foreign policy, and spoke of Britain's might and imperial destiny.

It was in his speech at the Crystal Palace later in 1872 that, in particular, he developed his themes, although he spoke firstly of the state of the party over the past generation:

1 A long period of power and prosperity had induced it to sink into a state of apathy and indifference ... the Tory system had degenerated into a policy which found an adequate basis on the principles of exclusiveness and restriction. Gentleman, the Tory Party unless it is a
5 national party is nothing. It is not a confederacy of nobles, it is not a democratic multitude; it is a party formed from all the numerous classes in the realm ... Now, I have always been of the opinion that the Tory Party has three great objects. The first is to maintain the institutions of the country ... Gentlemen, there is another ... object of the Tory Party
10 – to uphold the Empire of England ... Another great object of the Tory Party is the elevation of the condition of the people.

The health of the people [is] the most important question for a statesman. It involves the state of the dwellings of the people, the moral consequences of which are not less considerable than the
15 physical. It involves their enjoyment of some of the chief elements of nature – air, light and water. It involves the regulation of their industry, the inspection of their toil. It involves that purity of their provisions ... A leading member of the Liberal party described this ... as 'the policy of sewage'. Well, it may be the 'policy of sewage'
20 to a Liberal Member of Parliament. But to one of the labouring population ... it is not a 'policy of sewage', but a question of life and death ...

There was not much detail in his remarks, but their tone was inspirational, and they amounted to a shrewd bid by Disraeli for working-class support. Moreover, by 1872 the Liberals were appearing to lose their grip and the pendulum seemed to be swinging the Conservatives' way. The government had legislated impressively but deep divisions were now apparent. Some Liberals wanted more radical reform while the Whigs were troubled by Gladstone's desire for a continuing change. When Gladstone contemplated resignation in the hope that Disraeli and the Conservatives would take over, Disraeli was too wily to be trapped in this way. He wanted to see the government fall, but not until it had made itself even more unpopular and had suffered further setbacks in by-elections.

Eventually, a general election was called in 1874 and Gladstone's government was soundly defeated. It had trampled on too many vested interests and had offended too many groups. In particular, a substantial section of the wealthier middle classes switched their allegiance to Disraeli, whose promise of a more active foreign and imperial policy, and a rest from harassing legislation, appealed to them. An article in the *Fortnightly Review* by a contemporary Radical lamented that:

1 The real truth is that the middle class has swung round to Conservatism, of a vague and negative kind, for 'leaving well alone'. When we look at the poll in all the centres of middle-class industry, wealth and cultivation, we see that the rich trading class, and the com-
5 fortable middle class has grown distinctly Conservative.

Disraeli had given the party a more attractive image and had preached a new set of Tory ideals. He thought of them as being Tory because he disliked the use of the word 'Conservative' which seemed all too reminiscent of the policies of the 1830s and 1840s. Furthermore, he had appreciated that in a more democratic age elections could be decided by party organisation, and enough had been done to put the Tories into fighting shape (see pages 85 and 110–12). The party was now fit for government in a way that it had not been since the age of Peel. There were several able men in charge, armed with an improved organisation and a new policy. They formed the first majority Conservative government since 1841.

3 Disraeli's Second Ministry, 1874–80

> **KEY ISSUES** How effectively did the Conservatives undertake social reform? In what ways did Disraeli try to increase Britain's reputation in the world?

Disraeli was back in office for what was to be his last administration. In some ways his best years were past. As he later remarked, 'Ah, Power! It has come too late. There were days when, on waking, I felt I could move dynasties and governments; but that has passed away'. Now, he was beset by kidney disease, asthma and gout. Yet, despite his advancing years and physical decline, he was not out of touch with the needs of the time. He formed a strong government and, unlike Gladstone, he had a gift for gathering able young men around him. The Cabinet contained several new and talented ministers. Lord Salisbury (formerly Lord Cranborne) had been persuaded to serve, and Richard Cross became an energetic Home Secretary.

Power had come, but how would Disraeli use it? He had 'educated his party' and laid down general principles. He specialised in the broad sweep, but he could be tantalisingly vague on specifics. Ministers were left to fill in the details, and were alarmed to find that almost nothing was prepared by way of legislation.

a) Disraeli and Social Reform: His Early Outlook and Record

In his novels and in many of his speeches Disraeli had drawn attention to the shocking conditions in which millions of people lived. He had demanded that the government take firm action to put an end to these evils, and during the 1841 election, he had felt able to claim that 'there is no subject in which I have taken a deeper interest than the condition of the working class'.

The views expressed in those novels concerned the gulf between rich and poor. His publication of *Sybil; or the Two Nations* (1845) indicated his early approach, for in it he contrasted the two social classes which existed in England. On the one hand, there were riches and luxury, on the other, poverty and misery:

1 'Well, society may be in its infancy,' said Egremont, slightly smiling, 'but, say what you like, our Queen reigns over the greatest nation that ever existed.'
   'Which nation?', asked the stranger, 'for she reigns over two'.
5 The stranger paused; Egremont was silent, but looked inquiringly. 'Yes,' resumed the younger stranger after a moment's interval. 'Two nations; between whom there is no intercourse and no sympathy; who are as ignorant of each other's habits, thoughts and feelings, as if they were dwellers in different zones, or inhabitants of different planets; who
10 are formed by a different breeding, and are fed by a different food, are ordered by different manners and are not governed by the same laws.' 'You speak of – ' said Egremont, hesitatingly.
   'THE RICH AND THE POOR'.

Disraeli had an interest in social conditions, but was no crusader for improvement. Despite his observation in 1841, it would be misleading to think that this topic was ever one of his consuming preoccupations. He was dismayed at the worst aspects of working-class conditions, but did not often concern himself with the actual details of legislation. When important issues were debated in the House of Commons, he rarely spoke up for reform, and his voting record was patchy. On the Mines Act of 1842 he remained silent and abstained. He voted for the Ten Hour Bill of 1844, having spoken in the debate, and supported the Health of Towns Association, a pressure group for more sanitary towns and cities. He voted against renewal of the harsh New Poor Law, but on other questions did not seem to promote improvements, and frequently abstained in the lobbies.

Not until the 1860s and 1870s did he show a clear interest in and commitment to social reform. By then, personal preference and the search for political advantage seemed to go hand in hand. He felt that the party needed to champion social reform. He understood that the 'condition of the people' question was an important one, the more so after 1867. Reform would act as a bait for the newly-enfranchised voters. Concern for the welfare of the people would help his party at the polls, but beyond expediency, he also felt that social reform was a right and proper function for the Conservative Party and for the new generation of the aristocracy 'whose hearts are open to the responsibility of their position'. He believed in an hierarchical society, in which each class had its assigned role. He thought that the 'natural leaders of society', the gentlemen of England, would enjoy the trust of the people as long as they recognised these responsibilities. It was expedient to introduce reform, for as he put it, 'the palace is not safe, when the cottage is not happy'. But it was also a duty of the privileged orders to care for the happiness of the people.

It was a case stated in distinctly Tory terms. If its leaders acted appropriately, the gulf between the 'two nations' might be reduced, and the country might be more at ease with itself – although there would always be a variety of classes and interests. As Samuel Beer[4] has written:

1 Disraeli's Government of 1874 was Tory in both senses of the word; it
   was a time of strong government and its policies were rationalised by
   distinctively Tory purposes ... In Disraeli's version of Tory Democracy,
   a conception of authority was joined with a distinctive conception of
5 purpose ... Each class, rank and interest would enjoy security of status.

b) Disraeli's Premiership and Social Reform

In the 1874 election Disraeli's theme was essentially negative. He had promised a 'respite from the incessant and harassing legislation' of Gladstone and the 'dangerous' Liberals. He said little about reform other than to offer a general commitment. However, the impression given was that there would be a series of improvements, for after all, in his Crystal Palace speech, he had promised measures 'to elevate the physical as well as the moral condition of the people'. At one and the same time, he was a rallying point for those disturbed by excessive innovation and for those who wanted cautious, piecemeal reform. Therefore, he took office bound by no programme and committed to nothing specific; he was not the man for blueprints and carefully formulated schemes. But he did have a mandate to translate some of his general ideas into specific reform measures.

Some of his abler colleagues in the new Cabinet were surprised to find that he had no set ideas and no detailed policies to propose. There was a lack of direction from him and the conduct of affairs was left to individuals. Richard Cross recalled the situation in his memoirs:

1 When the Cabinet came to discuss the Queen's Speech, I was, I confess, disappointed at the want of originality shown by the Prime Minister. From all his speeches, I had quite expected that his mind was full of legislative schemes, but such did not prove to be the case; on the
5 contrary, he had to rely on the various suggestions of his colleagues,

and as they themselves had only just come into office, and that suddenly there, there was some difficulty in framing the Queen's Speech.

Sir Richard Cross, the Home Secretary, and formerly a successful Lancashire barrister and banker, deserves much of the credit for the reforms which were achieved. He was highly competent, a good administrator, and had a grasp of practical affairs. He represented a progressive vein of Conservatism. Inspired by Disraeli's utterances, he wanted to tackle the problems of people's living conditions, and he was the author of many of the reforms which were passed. In Cross's zeal for innovation, Robert Blake[5] has noted a resemblance to Neville Chamberlain's motivation. Chamberlain was to prove a reforming Conservative Health Minister under Stanley Baldwin in the 1920s.

c) The Main Reforms

Many industrial towns and cities contained large areas of insanitary back-to-back dwellings, and the Artisans Dwellings Act of 1875 attempted to deal with the problem of slum housing. Local authorities were empowered to purchase and demolish such property, and to reconstruct whole areas. Cross met with intense opposition from within his own party to a measure which was seen as an infringement of the rights of private property, and because of this he did not make the measure compulsory. Yet, despite its permissive character, in some parts of the country the Act was effectively employed, most notably in Birmingham. Joseph Chamberlain, the reforming Mayor of Birmingham, had discussed the Bill with Cross, and as a result the proposals had been improved. Using its terms, including the availability of cheap loans, Chamberlain produced a Birmingham Improvement Scheme which planned to clear away the slums near the city centre. However, in the process, he thwarted Cross's original intention that cheap working-class housing should be built, and instead embarked on a major programme of civic development, including the building of his new 'boulevard', Corporation Street.

Cross also took up the cause of public health, although it had been tackled by the Liberals. However, the legislation on the subject was still confusing, and needed to be rationalised so that the responsibilities of the various authorities were clearly specified. His Public Health Act (1875) was an important and far-reaching measure, for certain statutory duties were placed upon local councils – among other things, nuisances were to be removed, contaminated food safely destroyed and infectious diseases notified. Other items covered ranged from street-lighting to burials, and it remained the basis of legislation until 1929.

In the opinion of Liberal historian, R.K. Ensor,[6] 1875 was an *annus mirabilis* for useful domestic legislation. The Sale of Food and Drugs Act was designed to prevent the adulteration of food, and it laid down stringent regulations concerning the ways in which food was prepared. Again, this was a more comprehensive development of

Gladstonian legislation, extending its terms to cover more types of food and more types of shop. Purification was also the theme of another measure. A Rivers Pollution Act attempted to limit the offensive habit of discharging poisonous liquids and solid industrial waste materials into the waterways.

As part of the attempt to improve public health and living conditions, an effort was made to provide a healthier environment. The Enclosure Act protected the public's right to use the common pasture land by stopping landlords from absorbing it into their estates. Under this legislation, Epping Forest was saved for the people of London two years later.

The Agricultural Holdings Act was piloted by Disraeli himself, and was the first of its kind in mainland Britain. It provided displaced tenants with the right to compensation for improvements carried out on their land.

On factories, the 1874 Factory Act reduced the maximum working day to 10 hours and limited the week to 56 hours, allowing for a Saturday half-day. No child could work full-time until he or she was 14. The Factory and Workshop Act (1878) distinguished between a factory and a workshop, but ensured that both types of premises should be brought under regular governmental inspection. This was an important advance in the rights accorded to industrial workers.

The labour and trade-union legislation was an important breakthrough, pleasing employees and the unions. Disraeli anticipated that his new legislation would 'gain and retain for the Conservatives the lasting affection of the working classes'. The Conspiracy and Protection of Property Act of 1875 removed a grievance against Gladstone's government which had legalised trade unions but had denied them the right to engage in peaceful picketing. Cross now made picketing legal, and in a further Trade Union Act attempted to produce a clear definition of unions, and their rights and responsibilities. Old regulations against their activities were swept away.

His Employers and Workmen's Act redressed another grievance. Previously, if an employer broke a contract it was a civil wrong, which attracted only a light punishment, whilst if an employee committed the same offence, he could be charged with a breach of the criminal law. Both were put on the same footing, so that transgressions of the law were liable only to civil penalties.

By the Education Act of 1876 Lord Sandon sought to set up School Attendance Committees to ensure that children received an education. The duty was placed on parents of making sure that their children received adequate instruction, although the government did not specify that this must be given in schools. Similarly, the Committees could help parents of needy children with the payment of school fees, but did not have to do so.

Some of the other reforms were of little consequence, but one well-known act was brought about as a result of the activity of a private member, Samuel Plimsoll. Concerned that decrepit ships were often over-loaded by unscrupulous owners, so that if the ship went down they could claim (excessively) on their insurance, he persuaded the government to introduce a Bill. Reaction among the shipowners was very strong, and they waged a campaign of obstruction before the Merchant Shipping Act reached the statute book. From then on, a maximum load-line, the 'Plimsoll line', had to be marked on every ship.

In the last years of the ministry, dogged as it was by growing trade depression, Irish obstructionism in the House of Commons, and colonial problems, the impetus to reform drained away. Disraeli became ever more immersed in matters of foreign policy, and ministers and backbenchers were pleased to have a respite from further change.

d) Assessment of the Reforms

Disraeli's own attention was largely focused elsewhere, mainly in foreign affairs. He was prepared to offer his support for Cross's actions and took a general interest in them. In particular, he was much in sympathy with the labour legislation which Cross introduced. But he was not the architect of bills himself. Indeed, of the package of measures, some might have been brought forward whichever government was in power. For example, the Public Health Act was in the civil-service pipeline awaiting legislative action. Others such as the Pure Food and Drugs Act clarified the existing situation, and built on or modified previous laws. Few of the reforms actually broke new ground.

Moreover, not all of the reforms were as effective as they appeared on paper. Measures such as the Rivers Pollution Act were permissive not mandatory, so that local authorities could evade responsibility for implementing them if they so chose. Disraeli had long disapproved of compulsion, ever since his opposition to the centralising character of the New Poor Law of the Whigs. He explained his thinking in a speech on the Agricultural Tenants Bill:

1 Permissive legislation is the characteristic of a free people. It is easy to adopt compulsory legislation when you have to deal with those who only exist to obey; but in a free country, and especially in a country like England, you must trust to persuasion and example as the two great
5 elements, if you wish to effect any great changes in the manners of the people.

Blake[7] points out that by 1880, as a result of this approach, only 10 out of 81 local authorities had implemented the Artisans Dwellings Act. The government was setting down a standard, and progressive local authorities such as Birmingham derived much benefit from the opportunities available. Unfortunately, most did not perform so well.

Nonetheless, for most Conservatives the legislation went quite far enough and if Disraeli was to retain their backing he had to recognise their outlook and anxieties. Many of them still believed in *laissez-faire* and felt that government should uphold the rights of private property. Along with many Liberals, they were wary of intervention by the state, and preferred to stress self-reliance and self-improvement rather than collective action by the government on behalf of the community. Moreover, they had only a few years earlier criticised Gladstone for too much legislative action, which amounted to harassment of the voters in Conservative eyes. Even if they wanted to, they could hardly now opt for dramatic, sweeping changes which would have seemed far too exciting and controversial. This is why one backbencher described the measures introduced in 1875–6 as 'suet-pudding legislation ... flat, insipid, dull but ... very wise and very wholesome'.

These constraining factors were strengthened in the Conservative Party as a result of its changing social base. The Conservatives were the party of landed property, but in the 1870s many industrialists, factory and coal owners, had sought safe haven within their ranks; they had been frightened away from the Liberal Party by Gladstone's alleged radicalism. The party was now acting in defence of those who owned industrial and commercial property. These men were unlikely to favour measures to tackle social evils, such as long hours, low wages and other poor factory conditions. Such measures would have jeopardised their profits, and alienated their sympathies.

They were aware of the costs that reform might impose. They favoured low taxation, and particularly after 1876 the Chancellor was concerned to restrain expenditure. This limited scope for reform, for most changes in living and working conditions required public finance. This either came from taxes or the rates. As Conservatives often owned larger properties, they were concerned with any increase in their rate burden, and this limited action in areas such as education. In the traditionally Conservative rural areas, there was much alarm about local government expenditure.

These considerations meant that the social reforms passed between 1874 and 1880 were inevitably more modest in scope than might have been expected from a reading of Disraeli's early literature and speeches. Indeed, they were not even mentioned in the 1880 manifesto, which hardly suggests that the leadership attached great significance to them. Foreign policy was seen as far more important. Yet for all the limitations, they formed a worthwhile instalment of measures, ones of a scale and variety which 'root and consolidate a party'. Judged by sheer numbers, the list is impressive, but this, of course, says nothing of the measures' quality or lasting importance. In areas such as health, housing and the trade unions, the legislation was in advance of that of Gladstone, and was potentially of much benefit to those affected. Such considerations probably help to explain the much-quoted observation of one Lib-Lab MP, Alexander MacDonald, who remarked in a letter to *The Times* in 1879 that 'the Conservatives have done more for the working classes in five years than the Liberals have in fifty'.

Disraeli's rhetoric of 1872, if vague in character, was broadly fulfilled, for there had indeed been action to improve the 'conditions of the people'. His broad backing for changes suggests that he appreciated their significance, and his observations to contemporary confidants reflect this understanding. To Lady Bradford, speaking of particular reforms, especially of the Artisans' Dwellings Act, he stressed that they were important, 'because they indicate a policy round which the country can rally'. He was particularly impressed by Cross's labour reforms, for they fitted his conception of change perfectly, in that they did not involve government regulation, imposed no burden on the Exchequer, and, by giving the unions what they wanted, had settled 'the greatest question of the day; the relations between Capital and Labour'. Of the Employers and Workmen Act, he flattered the queen by telling her of his great pleasure that it had been passed on the anniversary of Coronation Day, and remarked that it settled 'the long-envenomed disputes between master and servant'. He thought that it was even more significant than the 1874 Ten Hours measure, 'which had had so beneficial an effect in softening the feelings of the working multitude'.

e) Disraeli and Overseas Policy

Earlier in his career Disraeli had not been an enthusiast for colonies, and had described them as 'millstones around our neck'. As late as 1866, he had written 'Leave the Canadians to defend themselves, recall the African squadron'. Yet in his Crystal Palace speech he had condemned the Liberals for their efforts, 'so continuous, so subtle, supported by so much energy, and carried on with so much ability and acumen, to effect the disintegration of the Empire of England'. By then, he seemed to be a keen advocate of Empire, perhaps seeing it as an issue on which to damage his opponents by impugning their patriotism. Furthermore, at a time when republican sentiment in the country was growing, the cry of Empire might rally people to the Throne as the symbol of an expanding country.

Disraeli's Crystal Palace speech offered little by way of detail, and his ideas on the Empire were generally thrown out somewhat casually and without a clear grasp of the actual issues. Although he is often credited with being the first front-rank British statesman to adopt a definite policy of imperial expansion, his policies do not match the image of him as a committed imperialist. He was always more concerned with the broad sweep or the bold imaginative stroke, than with the details of colonial settlement. His interest was sporadic rather than continuous, so that often he was in the position of reacting to events as problems arose, rather than initiating positive action himself.

His genuine interest was in India and the mysterious Orient. India, with its vast population of over 170 million, was a centre for trade, and an outlet for British goods and a source of valuable imports such as raw cotton, tea and wheat. More than this, it was the 'jewel in the Crown', for it offered the British governing classes a chance to show that they could successfully control native peoples and introduce them to Western ideas of civilisation. Because of this, governing India was a noble mission, and Disraeli was intent on preserving its safety, and the security of all routes to it.

He was able to perceive that a strong British Empire could stand firm in the world against any growing power; the Empire would thus be part of the reassertion of Britain's role and influence in the world. This imperial interest was evident in many events during his premiership, such as the annexation of Fiji, the purchase of the Khedive of Egypt's majority shareholding in the Suez Canal Company, and the annexation of the Transvaal. One of his most typical gestures was that which made the Queen 'Empress of India' in 1876. This was not a new idea, but one to which Gladstone had been noticeably unreceptive. It pleased Victoria, and was an indication of his wish to exalt the standing of an established British institution as well as of the importance he attached to the sub-continent.

Disraeli's first major biographers, Monypenny and Buckle,[8] discerned a 'genuine interest' in the Empire on Disraeli's part, and spoke of his 'prophetic vision'. Later historians have not been able to substantiate this and have shown his policy in office to be more of a series of improvisations and responses than a clear set of intentions. Fundamentally, he was not interested in the difficulties of particular colonies; what was more important was that these colonies were part of a powerful Empire taking its place in the world.

This was characteristic of Disraeli's entire approach to overseas affairs. Having criticised Gladstone's allegedly inactive and supine policy, he had no very specific ideas of his own. In 1874 he wanted to assert Britain's strength in Europe and in the world. He believed that Britain was isolated and in general decline, and he was determined to enhance Britain's greatness. His approach to questions of overseas policy was in some ways like that of Lord Palmerston. It was a tough, no-nonsense one, and one which was instinctively patriotic.

Disraeli was at the height of his reputation in 1878 on his return from Berlin, where a congress had taken place to resolve the Eastern Question and Russian claims to parts of the Ottoman Empire. He had achieved his aim of bringing about a halt to Russian aggression in the Balkans for the time being, and he had also gained a new acquisition for the British Empire, Cypress. He came home a popular hero, claiming to have brought back 'peace with honour'.

f) Defeat and Death

If an election had been called in 1878, Disraeli would almost certainly have been victorious, but the government had no reason to call one with two or three more years left before parliament must be dissolved. Over the following months the ministry's difficulties increased and as the time for an election drew nearer the outlook appeared less encouraging. Britain entered into the beginnings of the long depression which was to mark the last two decades of the nineteenth century, and in 1879 high unemployment was a serious problem. Disraeli had no answer to the demands of the Farmers' Alliance for some relief, and when his defeat came in the election he called in 1880 he claimed that 'hard times' had been responsible for undermining the reputation of his administration.

For the Opposition, however, this was not the key issue. Gladstone attacked the government's alleged 'impiety' in its handling of overseas matters, denouncing the failures of a 'forward' policy in the Transvaal and its actions in Afghanistan. He claimed that Disraeli had 'weakened the Empire by needless wars', and in his Midlothian Campaigns he poured invective upon the conduct of affairs. Disraeli was too old and too weary to answer the attack. He was unable to tour the country to restore enthusiasm. Similarly, his election address, with its warnings about Irish separatist demands, seemed to lack relevance to the immediate situation. Gladstone and the Liberals were more aware of the need to respond to the new electorate at this time, and their organisation was in vigorous fighting shape. By contrast, Conservative organisation was in decline after the improvements of ten years before. The outcome was a decisive defeat, in which the Conservatives lost support throughout the country, except in the South-east.

Disraeli had spent the years since 1876 in the House of Lords where he missed the lively atmosphere of the Lower House. By now, tired, lonely and often impassive, he was described as having 'lustreless eyes and face, like some Hebraic parchment', as he sat alongside Conservative peers. He continued to lead the party until his death in April 1881.

4 Assessment of the Disraelian Contribution

> **KEY ISSUES** What was the legacy of Disraeli to the late nineteenth century Conservative Party? Why do many Conservatives admire him today?

On Disraeli's death it fell to his arch-rival, Gladstone, to pay tribute to his qualities and his contribution to British political life. Gladstone anguished over his speech. Significantly, he preferred to dwell on some admirable personal qualities – 'his strength of will, his long-sighted consistency of purpose, reaching from his first entrance upon the avenue of life to its very close; his remarkable power of self-government, and, last, but not least of all, his great parliamentary courage' – rather than on his policies and achievements. In fact, Gladstone strongly disapproved of Disraeli and felt that he had debased the standard of political life. He saw him as opportunistic, unprincipled and lacking in the ethical sense which he believed to be so important. He could recognise that Disraeli had talents which set him above many other political figures but he objected to the way in which they were used to serve his own ambition and self-interest.

It is hard to deny the element of unscrupulousness and opportunism, traits noted by one of his successors, Lord Salisbury, who as the Earl of Cranborne, had so disliked the Second Reform Act of 1867. He described him as 'without principles and honesty ... in an age of singularly reckless statesmen, he is I think beyond question the one who is least restrained by fear of scruple'. Opportunism is a recurring charge in criticisms of Disraeli and the twists and turns of his career – in particular, his exploitation of the issue of protection – provide much evidence to substantiate it. However, some historians have sought evidence of an underlying consistency in his approach to public affairs. In as much as there was one, Lord Blake[9] believes it is to be found in his determination to maintain the position of the landed interest in British life. He quotes a letter Disraeli wrote to Lord Stanley in 1848 in which he describes the task of the official leader of the Conservative Party in the House of Commons as being 'to uphold the aristocratic settlement of the country'. He was referring not just to the great noble families, but to the social hierarchy found throughout rural England, including such bastions of the squirearchy as JPs and other substantial landowners.

Of course, it was among these 'gentlemen of England' that the party had its greatest strength at that time; it was in the county seats and in the small boroughs where the gentry had great influence that the Conservatives picked up most of their seats. Particularly after the Repeal of the Corn Laws, the party was primarily a party of the countryside. That element always remained, so that it is not surprising that Disraeli wished to preserve the 'aristocratic settlement'. However, at that time he was on occasion very dismissive about the squires who made up the parliamentary party, once referring to some who wished to speak in a debate as 'old trash'. Or again, he described some of the Tories soon after as 'destitute of ideas'. The fact is that he needed the landowners; they were the bulk of his party, and without them he was lost. In as much as he upheld their position, he was ensuring that he had a political future. His was a party of the land, and as Bruce Coleman[10] has written: 'The maintenance of the aristocratic constitution ... and the interests of landownership' were fundamental to mid-century Conservatism. However, Disraeli was prepared to ignore their advice when it seemed expedient to 'dish the Whigs' in 1867.

For all of Disraeli's failings, there is much which makes him appealing. He lacked the *gravitas* of Gladstone, with his deep moral fervour, and found his opponent something of a prig. Gladstone's style and manner can today seem very dated, for he was in many ways a typical Victorian. Disraeli's speeches, for all their classical allusions, can still be read today, and still sound lively. His colourful personality and his flair for self-dramatisation and publicity give him an extra appeal. He did not take himself too seriously, but suspected that the English people, 'being subject to fogs and possessing a large middle class, prefer grave statesmen'.

Disraeli was a fascinating character and the myth that has been woven around him only serves to heighten the interest. Few statesmen have remained so eminent in their reputation or possessed his attraction. He was only at the top of the pole with effective power for six years, and the scale of his achievements in office was good but not remarkable. But at different times he played out interesting roles, the outrageous and reckless adventurer, the tormentor of Peel, the man who claimed to have 'educated' his party, the supreme opportunist of the 1850s and 60s, the aged prime minister finishing his days in the House of Lords. As Robert Rhodes James[11] has observed: 'The deplorable young Disraeli had moved, by careful and deliberate metamorphosis, into the respectable Disraeli, the saviour of the Conservative cause, and [then] into the immortal Lord Beaconsfield'.

His reputation at the end of the nineteenth century was not high, but it was resurrected by Monypenny and Buckle[12] in their multivolume biography which first appeared in 1910. They were impressed by the Disraelian legacy, seeing him as the advocate of a strong overseas policy based on British interests, the defender of ancient institutions and a reforming Tory Democrat who was concerned to improve living conditions. Thereafter, there were few major assessments until Lord Blake produced his massive and important biography in 1966. Blake was clearly fascinated by his subject, but not uncritical, and ultimately found Disraeli's achievements to be more a matter of his style than of substance.

a) His Reputation Within the Modern Conservative Party

In 1883, on the anniversary of his death, some of his followers wore primroses in their lapels, as a mark of respect. From this gesture, there developed the Primrose League which was formed to spread his ideas and perpetuate his memory. In particular, it aimed to uphold 'religion, the estates of the realm and the imperial ascendancy'. Lord Randolph Churchill was much involved in its early history, and was to become a principal exponent of Tory Democracy, an elusive idea which was based on Disraelian attitudes and policies. In 1907, John Gorst attempted to define the policy of his former leader, saying:

i The principle of Tory Democracy is that all government exists solely for the good of the governed ... that all who are entrusted with any public function are trustees not for their own class, but for the nation at large; and that the mass of the people may be trusted so to use the electoral

5 power which should be freely conceded to them, as to support those who are promoting their interests. It is democratic because the welfare of the people is its supreme end; it is Tory because the institutions of the country are the means by which the end is to be attained.

Disraeli, though no modern democrat, would have echoed this spirit of 'Trust the People'. Since Gorst's time, many have placed much emphasis on his contribution to Tory Democracy, and he has become a figure of legend in the Conservative Party. For many decades, his very name provoked spontaneous applause from many people at Tory conferences who probably had only the barest acquaintance with what he actually did. They knew him to have been a Conservative hero, and mention of his name was a coded way of inviting listeners to bear in mind the 'One Nation' approach.

Initially, the Primrose League did much to foster that idea, so that the interests of the working classes were not overlooked. But in the short run, any progress in the direction of Tory Democracy was very limited, for Churchill's attempts to develop the tradition were swiftly terminated by his resignation in 1886 (see page 133). For several years after, the party's aristocratic old guard remained firmly in control, and Conservative policy lacked the bold Disraelian imprint.

However, in the twentieth century, much folklore grew up around his memory, and he has been seen, in *The Conservative Tradition*,[13] as the man responsible for 'that harmonious union, that magnificent concord of all interests, of all classes, on which our national greatness depends'. The Disraelian myth has clearly been a potent one, one which represents how many more progressive Conservatives like to see themselves. He has been credited with a degree of interest in living conditions which he never had, and his efforts at improvement were more spasmodic than Conservatives sometimes suggest.

Disraeli's contribution to Tory Democracy has been exaggerated, and bears only a loose resemblance to the facts of his career. If much has been made of his strengths, other aspects have been overlooked. His role in undermining the leadership over the repeal of the Corn Laws has been forgotten, even though it precipitated a major division which weakened the party for a generation. So too have some of his inconsistencies been erased from memory and examples of his opportunism have been downplayed. Often, his policies were pursued with a sharp eye to political advantage, and he was always more of a realist than an idealist, knowing what might be acceptable at any particular time.

Yet, despite all the reservations, he is an inspiration to Conservatives of a later generation. The more informed look back, unselectively sometimes, on what he wrote and did for justification of their own approach. For those who believe in using the power of the state to tackle social and economic problems, the Disraelian precedent provides a useful example. Several leaders have been keen to deny the idea that they have ever been members of a 'party of unbridled, brutal capitalism'. As a prominent post-war Conservative, Sir Anthony Eden, wrote: 'Although we believe in personal responsibility and personal initiative in business, we are not the political children of the *laissez-faire* school'.

However, it was Stanley Baldwin, the dominant inter-war Conservative, who was particularly fond of quoting Disraeli. He urged his supporters to work towards 'a further period of ordered progress in the tradition of that greatest of our leaders, Lord Beaconsfield'. This was an appropriate comparison for a Conservative leader to pursue in the world of the General Strike, when class conflict was acute. He was calling for a lessening of industrial tension and policies of national harmony, around which people could unite.

For Conservatives in later periods, the Disraelian mantle has been one they have wished to assume if they sought to unite the nation by policies of moderate reform and a lessening of social tension. Winston Churchill was able to claim that the acceptance of new policies in the 1950s was in the Tory tradition, and that the welfare state and managed economy were descended from 'the Tory Democracy of Lord Beaconsfield and after him, Lord Randolph Churchill'.

Baldwin, Butler, Macmillan and Heath can also claim descent from him. It was Edward Heath who, in defending the controversial 'Social Charter' of the European Community against its many critics, remarked that 'we Conservatives have possessed a social policy ever since Disraeli'. To advance such a view in the 1980s was less fashionable, for Margaret Thatcher was not seen as a soothing, healing leader; she made little use of the Disraelian legacy, and it was left to the so-called 'wets', her opponents in the party, to make use of the name of perhaps their most-quoted leader.

Disraeli did believe in the need for the Conservative Party to be broad-based in its appeal, and not to be the preserve of a single class. He was wise to recognise that 'the palace is not safe when the cottage is not happy'. His period at the top did give a new dimension to the party image and programme, equipping it with an element of social concern. His rhetoric was impressive, for he was a master of the political phrase, and Tory Democracy conjured up a useful image, the idea of a paternalistic aristocracy which looked after the working classes against the selfish interests of the rising industrial middle classes, just as he had outlined in *Sybil*. However, the actual content of his legislation hardly bears out the description, and as Blake[14] reminded us, it did not really involve a significant new departure in social policy; neither did it have much to do with his earlier philosophy.

Every party has figures from the past whom they regard with special affection. They are useful in that they show the link between modern politicians and those of an earlier period. For the Conservative Party, which prides itself on its roots in the past, they are of particular value, and the names of Pitt, Disraeli and Churchill are ones which still stand out today. Unlike Pitt, Disraeli was proud to call himself a Tory, so that his reputation has not been much disputed; no one in the party needs to justify his claim to a leading place in Conservative history.

b) Peel and Disraeli as Conservative Leaders

It is as 'One Nation' Disraelians, rather than as Peelites, that many Conservatives would like to portray themselves. As we have seen (see pages 71–3), Peel's name does not arouse great emotions, and he is less often seen as a party hero. One reason for this is obvious. For all of his good work in recreating the Conservative Party, Peel is seen as the man who by mishandling of the Corn Law issue dealt it a devastating blow which ruined it for a generation. Even though Disraeli was the architect of his fall and played a leading part in opening up that split, his memory shines more brightly. For, although he was defeated in 1880, he left the party in an altogether healthier condition, so that it was in a position to compete on favourable electoral terms and to dominate the period which followed.

Disraeli pursued his aims with more panache, more political skill, and more concern for party unity. However, in some ways the two men's contributions were remarkably similar. Both were in the business of educating their party to new conditions. Peel after 1832 and Disraeli after 1846 were leading a party which was at a low ebb in its fortunes. New vigour and a change of image were essential if survival was to be assured. Both saw the need for the party to adapt and to come to terms with a changing situation.

However, they represented different strands of party tradition. Disraeli found Peelite Conservatism not at all to his liking, for it placed too little emphasis on safeguarding those institutions he so much revered, was not rooted in principle, and was too willing to accommodate itself to change. Moreover, the ideas they propounded were different. Peel was concerned to broaden the party's backing to cater for the new middle classes who had become a dominant force and whom Disraeli much despised. Disraeli's dream, from the time of his Young England days, harked back to an earlier age. He spoke of a party led by a patrician landed element with a sense of duty, which had a care for, and an appeal to, voters in the industrial towns.

As Professor Gash[15] has noted, a curious feature of the Conservative party is that, although its practice has almost invariably been Peelite, in that it developed to become a party of the middle-class men of landed, commercial and industrial property, its myth has been Disraelian. Disraeli imparted the idea that Conservatism, led by a wealthy aristocracy with a sense of concern for the whole nation, could survive into a more democratic age. It need not fear the extension of the franchise. If Tory Cabinets of the twentieth century appear to have been Peelite in their composition, the language of many of the party leaders has been based on the Disraelian legacy; respect for ancient institutions allied to an approach which speaks of the broadest national interests, rather than those of their own more wealthy supporters.

A Note on … Party organisation

After the repeal of the Corn Laws, the main institutional elements of the party at first remained in Peelite hands. Key figures were on Peel's side, and the Party Fund was used to back Peelite candidates. Soon, the structure created in the 1830s fell into decline and disuse, as the Peelite forces gradually lost their cohesion. Bonham, the Principal Agent, disappeared from political life.

a) Developments outside the House, 1846–67

The rump of the Conservatives toyed with the idea of a change of name because their title was so closely associated with Peel. They thought of calling themselves Protectionists, but within a few years the label had ceased to be appropriate. The 'Country Party' was a possibility, but the leadership feared that either term might serve as a barrier to would-be recruits. 'Conservative' had a more national appeal, and its continued use seemed to keep the door ajar to the Peelites.

The former Protectionists had to start almost from scratch, for they possessed no organisation and no funds. It is because the party had to be relaunched in 1846 that Lord Blake[16] dates the Conservative Party from this date, for although the name can be traced to the early thirties, the organisation cannot: 'From every aspect of institutional continuity whether as a party within Parliament or outside, 1846 is a better year of birth than 1832 or 1833'.

In 1852 Disraeli decided to put more vigour into the party organisation. As a result of the changes he made, power was vested with the leadership, the whips and in the Carlton Club. This was the era in which 'club politics' flourished, for apart from the Carlton Club, situated in Pall Mall, since 1840 there had been the Conservative Club which served as a substitute for those who could not gain entry into the over-subscribed Carlton, and in 1864 a less-exclusive Junior Carlton Club was formed. This catered for what Disraeli called 'the working corpus of our party', by which he meant the professional men, the 'country attorneys and agents who want a political and social focus in London'. By then, the influence of the Carlton Club had already passed its heyday, but it was still much used by grandees from the rural constituencies. In the more urban areas, the gentry were less involved in Conservative politics, and often it was a local solicitor who carried out the important task of organising the registration of voters. A new Conservative Registration Association was founded in 1863 to co-ordinate their work.

b) Developments Outside the House after 1867

After 1867, the idea of branches in the constituencies supporting the parties in the House of Commons received a new impetus, and whereas in the past general elections had often been fought at the local level on matters of purely local concern, this was no longer to be the case. With the vote extended to so many workingmen, parties needed to organise their support. Much of the initiative for this came from the politicians at Westminster who hoped that they would be able to influence and control the new electors so that an age of increasing democracy would not result in the rise of extremism. Gradually, organised activity spread outwards from London into the country, based on the party headquarters co-ordinating the work of many associations.

In 1867 the electorate increased from 1.36m to 2.46m, and the bulk of the additional voters were from the working classes of the towns and cities. The Birmingham Liberals, with much help from the young Joseph Chamberlain, had been quick to see the opportunities created by the Reform Act, but following their successful example many associations were formed by both parties up and down the country. Often based on the old Registration Societies, these associations were expected to 'nurse' constituencies between elections and to organise support during them. New techniques of persuasion were required, and this involved a greater emphasis upon explaining policy, via manifestoes and speechmaking tours. Leaflets were handed out and voters were carefully canvassed so that on election day the maximum party vote could be mobilised.

In addition to the new associations, several Conservative workingmen's organisations were created, places where working-class voters could have a drink and a game of billiards, and make their contribution to local party activity. They were usually clubs rather than associations, and it was the latter which were linked by the National Union of Conservative and Constitutional Associations, set up in 1867. Some people still had doubts about the word 'Conservative', hence the addition to the name, which had the added advantage of seeming to imply that opponents were, by definition, 'unconstitutional'. Altogether, there were spokesmen from 55 constituencies at the meeting which established the National Union, the purpose of which was 'to consider by what organisation we may make Conservative principles effective among the masses'.

The National Union did not seek a say in determining the

party programme, and at its 1873 Conference one of its founders stressed that it had been 'organised rather as ... a handmaid to the party, than to usurp the functions of party leadership'. It got off to an inauspicious start. No ministers attended its inaugural gathering and there was some anxiety in the constituency associations that they would lose their identity and independence in this larger creation. It was the arrival of John Gorst as one of its Joint-Secretaries which gave its status and fortunes a boost. He had chaired the meeting in 1867 at which it was launched and had become Party Agent in 1870. He was an industrious and able organiser who had a genuine belief in the concept of the Conservative workingman, and was keen to develop the party's appeal in the urban areas. He saw Disraeli's Tory Democracy as an attractive creed to sell to the new electorate, and Disraeli himself helped him enhance the reputation of the National Union by choosing to make his two big speeches in 1872 at its regional and national conferences.

The Union was the mass organisation which represented the party in the country. New machinery was needed at the centre, in London, to manage the next campaign, so that there could be the best possible back-up for candidates in the field, by way of propaganda, speeches and funds. Conservative Central Office was established in 1870, though it did not acquire this name for another year. It set out to improve the number and quality of candidates, and by 1874 the Conservatives were in fighting shape. Their superior organisation contributed to the scale of their victory, for they were fielding more candidates than they had ever done before and these men were better supported from headquarters.

In 1872 the two new national organisations moved into the same building, and Central Office became a powerful headquarters from which to arrange future party election campaign and to co-ordinate activity in the country. Disraeli's reforms had established the broad pattern of Conservative organisation which exists today – in parliament, the leadership and the Whips: outside, the Conservative headquarters at Central Office and a network of associations around Great Britain.

References

1 Lord Blake, *The Conservative Party from Peel to Major* (Heinemann, 1997)
2 I. Machin, *Disraeli* (Longman, 1995)
3 I. Machin, *Disraeli*
4 S. Beer, *Modern British Politics* (Faber and Faber, 1969)
5 Lord Blake, *The Conservative Party from Peel to Major*

6   R. Ensor, *England 1870–1914* (OUP, 1963)
7   Lord Blake, *The Conservative Party from Peel to Major*
8   W. Monypenny and G. Buckle, *The Life of Benjamin Disraeli, Earl of Beaconsfield,* (2 vols,1929)
9   Lord Blake, *The Conservative Party from Peel to Major*
10 B. Coleman, *Conservatism and the Conservative Party in Nineteenth Century Britain* (Arnold, 1988)
11 R. Rhode James, *The British Revolution* (Methuen, 1978)
12 W. Monypenny and G. Buckle, *The Life of Benjamin Disraeli, Earl of Beaconsfield*
13 R. White, 'The Conservative Tradition' in P. Buck, ed., *How Conservatives Think* (Penguin, 1975)
14 Lord Blake, *The Conservative Party from Peel to Major*
15 N. Gash, *Sir Robert Peel* (Longman, 1986)
16 Lord Blake, *The Conservative Party from Peel to Major*

Summary
The Predominance of Disraeli, 1846–81

Tories in Wilderness to 1866	Rise of Disraeli to Real Power	Disraeli in Office 1874–80
1846 Repeal of Corn Laws	1846 Repeal of Corn Laws	1874 Victory
Tory split – Peelites: some drift over to Liberals, some remained Protectionists	Emergence as leader of Protectionists	Policy of 'Empire, Monarchy and Social Reform'
Protectionists become Conservative Party	Seized chance, 1867, to pass Parliamentary Reform	Package of social measures, 1874–6
Derby led Minority govts 1852 1858–9 1866–8	1868 PM	Assertion of British interests abroad
Passage of Parliamentary Reform, 1867	1872 Crystal Palace speech	1880 Election defeat
	1874 Election victory	

Working on Chapter 4

Your work on this chapter should cover three issues:

1. the personality and character of Benjamin Disraeli,
2. the domestic achievements of Disraeli's second ministry and
3. Disraeli's effect on the Conservative Party, both i) during his lifetime and ii) subsequently.

When you carry out the first task make sure that you indicate i) the way in which opinions on this have differed, and ii) the ways in which Disraeli changed through his lifetime.

The second task will require a listing of the main reforms passed by parliament between 1874 and 1880. For each reform make a comment about its i) strengths, and ii) weaknesses. How much should Disraeli be credited for what was achieved?

You could approach the third task as two distinct activities. It might be a good idea to write about the first part in two 'periods'. What should be the dividing date between the periods? Would it be helpful to consider the second part of this issue in periods? If you adopt this approach, the last period should end in 1979. Why is this?

Answering structured and essay questions on Chapter 4

The most obvious subject for structured questions on Disraeli is his second ministry. Look at this example:

a) What were the main social reforms passed during the first years (1874–6) of Disraeli's second ministry?
b) In what ways did these reforms improve the lot of working people?
c) How should credit and blame for the reforms' strengths and weaknesses be apportioned?

It is likely that you have had plenty of practice answering questions such as a) and b). What is the examiner looking for in answers to this type of question? Question c) is very demanding, largely because it is not easy to work out exactly what the question requires you to do. Discuss with others the way in which you would organise an answer to this question. Is there any place in the answer for a consideration of the criteria to be used in making judgments about credit and blame?

Essay questions are likely to range more widely and be more provocative. Consider the following:

1. 'Disraeli did more harm than good to the Conservative Party.' Discuss.
2. Has Disraeli's contribution to the development of the Conservative Party been exaggerated?
3. Was Disraeli as unscrupulous as many of his opponents alleged?

4. 'Disraeli made virtually no contribution to the social-reform programme of his second ministry, 1874–80.' Do you agree?

Remember that when you are answering questions that are essentially of the 'challenging statement' type, as the four examples above are, you should always seek to present both sides of the argument. Naturally, you will normally want to support one point of view, but you must ensure that interpretations you do not support are given full treatment. Which of the questions would be most difficult to answer by giving both sides of the argument? How would you do it?

Source-based questions on Chapter 4

1. The State of the Tory Party in the Period 1846–60

Study the cartoon on page 80 and the extracts on pages 85 and 89 and answer the following questions:

a) Note the date of the cartoon and suggest reasons why *Punch* appears to have a low opinion of Disraeli. (*2 marks*)

b) What do you understand by *The Times* reference to 'the hopeless state' of the Conservative Party when Disraeli became one of its leaders? (page 89, line 1) (*3 marks*)

c) To what extent do the two extracts agree on Disraeli's contribution to the revival of the party? (*5 marks*)

d) Why might a historian of the Conservative or Tory Party in this period value the evidence of these two extracts and yet wish to treat them with caution? (*5 marks*)

e) Using your own knowledge of the topic and the evidence in these two extracts how far do you agree that 'in the period after the Repeal of the Corn Laws and through to the 1868 election Disraeli saved the Conservative Party'? (*10 marks*)

2. Disraeli in Opposition, 1872

Read the extracts on pages 93 and 94 and answer the following questions:

a) From the second extract identify and explain the significance of the 'three great objects' Disraeli saw as important to the Tory party (page 94, line 8). (*6 marks*)

b) How, judging by these extracts, did the purpose and the nature of the Crystal Palace speech differ from that given by Disraeli in Manchester? (*3 marks*)

c) Explain your understanding of Disraeli's comment 'the Tory Party unless it is a national party is nothing' (page 94, lines 4–5). (*4 marks*)

d) Using your own knowledge explain why these two speeches were so important to the revival of the Tory party. (*12 marks*)

5 The Era of Salisbury and Balfour, 1881–1914

POINTS TO CONSIDER

After 1885, there were nearly two decades of Conservative majorities in the House of Commons. Party success or failure at this time had much to do with the impact of the Irish Question (see pages 126–8 and 129–31), which inflicted heavy damage on the Liberals. They lost key figures such as Joseph Chamberlain who joined up with the Salisbury-led Conservatives. Under the leadership of Balfour (1902–6), the Conservatives themselves were in difficulty and in 1906 the party suffered one of its worst-ever results. Electoral fortunes improved in 1910, but on the eve of the First World War there was little evidence that the party was ready for office.

As you read this chapter, think carefully about the role of key figures such as Lord Randolph Churchill, Joseph Chamberlain, Lord Salisbury and Arthur Balfour. What were their different priorities and how well did they work together? Consider the features which the Disraelian and post-Disraelian party had in common. You should then be in a position to assess whether the influence of Disraeli long survived his passing.

KEY DATES

1881	Death of Disraeli.
1885	Lord Salisbury formed his first administration.
1886	Salisbury formed his second administration: Churchill resigned.
1892	Defeat of the Conservatives.
1895	Salisbury formed third administration, which included Liberal Unionists.
1899	Chamberlain, as Colonial Secretary, led Britain into Boer War.
1900	Khaki election won by the Conservatives.
1902	Salisbury resigned, his nephew Balfour took over.
1906	Conservative debacle at the polls.
1906–14	Years of impotence and frustration.
1911	Replacement of Balfour by Bonar Law.

1 Three Leading Conservative Personalities

KEY ISSUES What were the main differences in the style, approach and policy attitudes of Lord Randolph Churchill and Lord Salisbury? How was it that the ex-Radical Joseph Chamberlain could be won over to the Conservative side?

Defeat in 1880 indicated that the Conservatives had lost their appeal to the voters and for the first few years of opposition there was little sign that they would be back in office within a short time. The party was led in the House of Commons by Sir Stafford Northcote and in the Lords by Lord Salisbury. From the beginning, the leadership was a cause of dispute. Northcote was ineffectual, his long-winded speeches making little impact upon MPs. He was no match for Gladstone, and several Conservatives wanted to see a more dynamic attack on the Liberal government. Lord Beaconsfield shared some of the misgivings, even though he admired the leader's general efficiency. He told one dissident MP that members should 'stick to Northcote. He represents the respectability of the party. I wholly sympathise with you all, because I was never respectable myself'. He went on to advise the individual not to 'break with Northcote, but defer to him as often as you can'.

Doubters saw Northcote as too cautious and responsible, and they disliked his excessive gentility. He was a figure of fun, much mocked for his high-pitched voice. Among his more unsparing and persistent critics was Lord Randolph Churchill, who in private mocked him as 'The Goat', on account of the shape of his head, or as the 'GOW', the Grand Old Woman, as opposed to Gladstone who was the Grand Old Man.

a) Lord Randolph Churchill

Lord Randolph Churchill had entered the House of Commons in 1874 as the Conservative MP for the family borough of Woodstock. He came from a privileged background, born at Blenheim Palace, the son of the seventh Duke of Marlborough. He was educated at Eton and Oxford. In the House he aroused the curiosity and admiration of those around him. As a politician, he was well-equipped, possessing boundless self-confidence, a colourful personality and a brilliant debating style. Slight in build, he was to become a giant among parliamentarians. He was irrepressible and audacious, specialising in satirical speech. He devastatingly used his wit to savage the Gladstone administration on several fronts, notably the government's handling of Irish affairs and Egyptian policy.

He was also a regular critic of his own party's leadership, and frequently overshadowed the Tories on his own Front Bench. He wanted them to assault Gladstone with more vigour and boldness but, above all, he wished to rally his supporters and turn Conservatism into a popular movement. Within the House, he and three others formed themselves into a 'ginger group' which often took a bold and independent line. The four men devoted much of their time to taunting and embarrassing Gladstone, but they also advanced their own creed of Tory Democracy. It had far more appeal than the policies pursued by the Front Bench which seemed to lack ideas and inspiration.

When a member of the House stated that 'there are two great

ATHWART THE COURSE.

Randolph Churchill (an approaching Bay). "IN THE WAY AGAIN! 'OORAY!!"

Randolph Churchill and other members of the Fourth Party were very effective in attacking the Gladstone government, making it difficult for ministers to chart a steady course.

parties in the state', it was Parnell, the leader of those Irish MPs favouring Home Rule, who shouted out 'three', thereby prompting Churchill to cap this with 'four'. The label caught on, for many contemporaries recognised that those in the group did behave as an independent force. Throughout the life of the Liberal ministry their destructive talents were used to goad their own Front Benchers as much as those on the opposite side. The witty, irreverent and half-conspiratorial appeal of the Fourth Party has been compared to that of the Young England group of which Disraeli had been such a prominent member. Both groups disliked the leaders of the party, but whilst the one advocated a radical Toryism, the other stressed the need for democratic Conservatism. Neither much liked the consensual approach, as represented by Peel and Northcote.

b) Churchill and Tory Democracy

Churchill's involvement established his reputation as a Conservative with a future, but his attention was not limited to the House of Commons; neither was his popularity. He wished to see Conservatism develop as a popular movement in the country, and to this end he was prominent in the formation of the Primrose League in 1883, and in attempts to democratise the organisation of the Tory Party (see pages 149–50). He attempted to give meaning and substance to the Disraelian concept of Tory Democracy. However, his observations were rarely very helpful in amplifying it. In 1884, he made the classic non-statement that 'Tory Democracy is a democracy which supports the Tory Party'.

He had elaborated his views a little more lucidly a year earlier in the *Fortnightly Review,* when he had clearly placed himself in the Disraelian tradition, claiming that Tory Democracy was a direct descendant of *Sanitas sanitatum, omnia sanitas.* He saw the Toryism of the 1870s as being 'a scheme of social progress and reform, of dimensions so large and wide spreading that many volumes would not suffice to explain its details'. He wished to continue that tradition, and as a great coiner of popular phrases, was able to attract attention. The phrases sounded impressive, but the content was often unclear. Tory Democracy remains vague and elusive despite his attempted explanation.

He possessed general ideas on policy but they did not amount to a comprehensive programme. The nearest he came to setting one out was to be in his Dartford Speech in 1886. His proposals included land reform to benefit the recently-enfranchised agricultural labourer, including measures to change the agricultural rating system and cheapen the costs of land transfer. He also favoured a reconstruction of local government in the counties, changes in parliamentary procedures and economy in government expenditure so that taxation could be reduced. As a Conservative, he was not in a position to propagate bold and expensive social reforms, for these would have seemed threatening to the pockets and property of those members of the upper and middle classes, whose support the party needed to retain. On the one hand, he had to appeal to the aspirations of the conservative middle classes, and on the other to the instincts of the working classes for reform. It was a difficult balancing act for a reforming Tory.

What Churchill lacked was a new economic policy. In the Liberal Party, Chamberlain and fellow Radicals in the early 1880s could win votes by denouncing landlordism, from which they were economically independent. As Lord Blake[1] has observed, there was no comparable interest of which the Conservatives could make a scapegoat. Both landlords and big business had too strong a hold in the Conservative Party. Perhaps the best tactics would have been to think in terms of social insurance on the Bismarckian (German) model, but the Conservatives showed no understanding of such a policy. 'Tory Democracy' remained a fine phrase and not a policy, for Churchill was unable to think outside of his own class even when the demands of the party struggle made this desirable. It was neither a realistic doctrine, nor a carefully thought-out programme of reform. Indeed, to Lord Rosebery, a Liberal opponent, it was an 'imposture'.

Yet Churchill's speeches and actions were a tonic to the demoralised Tories and, ultimately, it is not for its content but rather for its understanding of the need to be popular that the Tory Democracy of the Fourth Party is remembered. Lady Gwendoline Cecil,[2] the daughter of Lord Salisbury, understood this well. She observed that Churchill saw the necessity for a popular variety of Conservatism, and the need for the party to communicate its ideas: 'It was not the creed of Conservatism that they doubted, but its power of appeal to the electorate'.

Churchill often spoke of the 'traditional institutions' of the country, just as Disraeli had done, but he found it impossible to explain how their survival would enhance the welfare of the people. In another headline-catching phrase, he wanted to 'trust the People', in the expectation that that they would place their trust in such 'natural rulers' as himself. He emphasised that this had long been part of his philosophy, and that his purpose was 'to rally the people round the Throne, to unite the Throne with the people, a loyal Throne and a patriotic people, that is our policy and that is our faith.' Quoting another Churchill observation – when in a cynical and flippant aside he described Tory Democracy as 'mostly opportunism' – Blake[3] concludes that '[his] position really depended less on any policy or programme than on brilliant opposition demagoguery'. His career, like that of the Fourth Party which he dominated, was to be brief and dazzling. His ultimate purpose was to launch a bid for the leadership, but he underestimated the power of resistance of the Old Guard as represented by Lord Salisbury.

c) Lord Salisbury: Personality and Qualities

Lord Salisbury was officially declared Conservative leader in 1885 when he formed his first administration. He remained in that position until 1902, yet despite the longevity of his period at the head of his party, including three spells as Prime Minister, his impact on the Conservative Party and its evolution was not very great. Whereas Disraeli achieved a lasting place in Conservative affection, and Lord Randolph Churchill achieved fame (or notoriety) in a career which was over almost before it had begun, Lord Salisbury has left no striking memorial – despite being, in Winston Churchill's words, 'venerable, august Lord Salisbury, Prime Minister since God knows when'. He did little to arouse popular enthusiasm and probably had no wish so to do. For much of his period in office he was carried by events rather than being in control of them.

The other two men were picturesque personalities, whereas Salisbury lacked the attributes needed to become a popular leader. Neither did he command the moral authority of a Gladstone. His was a dignified presence, instantly recognisable by his beard and, if he lacked both eloquence and personal magnetism, he could nonetheless speak effectively when roused by the issues which Gladstone took up. He managed to speak on 70 public platforms between 1880 and 1886.

He was an aristocrat living in a democratic age. Yet he was also a realist with a fine intelligence and a tremendous sense of public duty. He remained aloof and regarded life's successes and failures with a cynical detachment. To him man's journey often seemed an improbable one, and he was unsure to what end it was directed. He believed that as long as one did one's duty, the responsibility for the result rested with God. He couldn't possibly pretend to understand the modern world, for as he said: 'We live in a small bright oasis of knowledge surrounded on all sides by a vast unexplored region of impenetrable mystery'. As Peter Marsh[4] points out: '… a sense of living in a beleaguered enclave, of having to keep the forces of hostile barbarism at bay, pervaded his mature outlook'.

He held firm views on issues of political principle, and he disliked the extension of the franchise. As Lord Cranborne he had opposed Disraeli in 1867, advancing the view that 'first-rate men will not canvass mobs, and mobs will not elect first-class men'. He was frankly sceptical of democracy, and given his negative approach and reactionary views it does seem strange that he should have been Prime Minister for so long. Of course, it is probable that he would not have been so but for the schism over Home Rule which caused the Liberal Party to disintegrate. Yet he was also a realist, with sufficient political good sense to accept the inevitable and to make the best of it. Although he often opposed changes which he thought were unwise, he accepted them once they had been implemented.

In some respects, his personality was not without appeal. Despite his background he disliked upper-class society, even though he could be a charming host. He despised much of the superficiality and shallowness of its members, and was scornful of the sham of the world he inhabited. Yet he was resigned to his fate, for the 'usual destiny of us unfortunate white slaves' was to be 'stressed and bored at dinners and at parties'. He was by preference a solitary man, and resented the effort of society to interfere with his privacy. He loved to play with mechanical contrivances, particularly the telephone, and was known to startle his house guests by unexpectedly calling 'hey, diddle diddle' down the line – just as he was by suddenly switching off the lights, a new ploy made possible by the coming of electricity.

He was undoubtedly a keen Christian, but mixed up with his religious convictions was a blend of cynicism and fatalism. He was a devout Anglican, and the Church of England had his unswerving loyalty. But his views were not of the sort to appeal to those who liked their religion to be clear-cut and uncomplicated, and his daughter observed that throughout his life he found it hard to accept the moral teaching of the Gospels. He experienced difficulty in fathoming life's meaning – 'God is all-powerful and God is all-loving – and the world is what it is! How are you going to explain that?'.

d) Salisbury and Social Change

Salisbury believed in the traditional, early nineteenth-century 'Church and King' Toryism. He believed that existing institutions should be changed only as far as was necessary to remedy proven deficiencies. Like Burke, he doubted the value of legislation based on planning for the future, for 'large conceptions in law-making are characterised by their disregard of justice and individual liberty, or their sacrifice of realities to the symmetry of cherished theories'.

For him, the primary business of government was to administer the existing order, and the Conservatives owed their first duty to the classes who relied upon them to defend their interests. He was 'anxious to make this country more pleasant to live in for the vast majority of those who live in it ... [and to] diminish the divergences between classes'. In a general sense, therefore, he was keen on the idea of better living conditions, particularly in housing and the provision of free education. However, such proposals as he made for social reforms were limited by the firm conviction that it was essential to respect private property and do nothing which would weaken self-reliance.

He had little faith in the idea of betterment by legislation, and doubted the power of political action to improve the world. The things that were wrong in life were primarily faults of human nature, and there was little the politicians could do to make men and women better. He had a sombre distrust of any notion of social and economic change. For years, he had battled to check the advance of democracy, and shortly after the great defeat of 1867, he became worried about the advance of socialism, which he described as 'a decorous form of pillage'. He was worried about the future and the threat posed by this and other creeds which threatened the stability of society as it had long been known. He believed that socialists were motivated not by 'a philanthropic spirit, but by a mere impulse of class antipathy'.

Salisbury was described in 1892 as the 'Prime Minister of despair whose plan was to accept as inevitable whatever system he found existing', and it was true that he had spent much of his political life fending off change. When explaining his party's attitude to the abolition of church rates, he spoke of what had been gained by the approach he had adopted: 'Even if the Tories are defeated, at any rate, we have obtained delay, and delay is life'. His fears were less intense later in his life, and the Disraeli premiership had shown what could be achieved by a Conservative leader. The image of Conservatism as a national creed, appealing to all sections of the community, had an attraction, as long as achieving this did not involve such an active role for the state that individual liberty was in jeopardy.

Nonetheless, Marsh[5] concludes that at the root of Salisbury's politics was fear:

1   The threatening aspect of the world as Salisbury saw it made him a fighter. Though he had no faith that things would improve, though he was contemptuous of optimism, he could not rest in in-action. Not quite despairing, he fought; when he lost, he would be plunged into
5   gloom, only to rise and fight again.

Marsh's view is endorsed in the recent biography of Andrew Roberts.[6] He also detects an 'innate fatalism' in Salisbury's character, a sense that the landowning aristocracy and the Church of England, would eventually be brought down by a burst of destructive radicalism. But despite this appalling possibility, it was probably worth one more effort to stave off the apocalypse. Roberts quotes Salisbury's own portrayal of himself as a policeman whose task was to frustrate 'the workers of mischief'. Among those mischievous workers were the members of the new London County Council which he described in 1894 as 'the place where a new revolutionary spirit finds its instruments and collects its arms'!

This essentially pessimistic man presided over the fortunes of the Conservative Party at the very time when Churchill was trying to democratise it. The difference in style between the two men is evident, one urging his colleagues to 'trust the People', the other having a fear of the masses and their potential to change the balance of society as he wanted it to remain. For Salisbury, it was a matter of the aristocracy holding onto the reins of power for as long as possible. In the long term, it was probably doomed to lose its rearguard action, but in the meantime he was determined to stave off the evil hour. This was the task to which he devoted his political life and he was surprisingly successful in achieving it during the years of his premiership. As evidence of this, we only have to look at his electoral record. He led the party through three impressive victories in 1886, 1895 and 1900, whilst his defeats in 1885 and 1892 were ones which left the Liberals in office rather than in power.

It is this record which has led Michael Bentley[7] to portray Salisbury as 'the most formidable politician the Conservative Party has ever produced'. It is a remarkable and probably over-stated claim, the more so as for much of the time, his was a policy of negation. As for the impressive performance in close-of-century elections, there were several factors which helped the Party to triumph at the polls. The popularity of Salisbury and his vision of defensive Conservatism was probably rather less significant than the state of the contemporary Liberal Party (see the box on pages 127–9).

Salisbury showed some skill in exploiting the mood of the time, by ensuring that people of property could find a safe haven under the Conservative umbrella. But in an age when the franchise was being extended, his policies offered little incentive to the majority of working men to join them. Whereas Disraeli was aware of the need to unite the 'two nations' and ensure that the party had a wide appeal, Salisbury saw them as having divergent interests. He had little understanding of the 'condition of the people' question and of its political significance. Instead of wooing the working classes, he preferred to target the middle classes, which Disraeli had neglected. For Salisbury, 'villa Toryism' was something to be cultivated, and this approach found a welcome among the supporters of the family affair that was the contemporary Conservative leadership, often known at the time as the 'hotel Cecil'.

e) Joseph Chamberlain and the Liberal Unionists

The Liberal split over Home Rule had left Lord Hartington and Joseph Chamberlain, as Liberal Unionists, in the political wilderness. They were unlikely bedfellows, possessing very different personalities and ideas. Hartington was perhaps the last great Whig patrician to play an active part in English politics. His seeming indolence and inertia, his distaste for popular politics and legislation, and his innate caution were in marked contrast to Chamberlain's approach. Chamberlain had made his reputation as a hard-hitting Radical. He had been a reforming mayor of Birmingham (1873–6), and was noted for his drive and determination to get things done. He possessed a flair for party organisation and was prominent in the local Liberal 'caucus'. This term, literally meaning a 'meeting of wire pullers', was the one used by critics of the Birmingham Liberal Federation, of which Chamberlain was a prominent member. They disliked his alleged 'Americanisation' of political activity, and his professional approach to canvassing supporters and setting out programmes.

His programme of speech making around the country culminated in the publication of his Unauthorised Programme of 1885. In it, he suggested a policy of land reform, to provide allotments and smallholdings for the benefit of agricultural labourers, graduated income

JOSEPH CHAMBERLAIN 1836–1914, THE CONSERVATIVE AND UNIONIST PERIOD — *-Profile-*

1886	Broke with Gladstone over Home Rule, became a Liberal Unionist
1887	Failure of Round-Table talks aimed at bringing about a Liberal reunion
1887–92	Liberal Unionists drew closer to the Conservative Party
1895	Became Colonial Secretary in Salisbury's Third Administration
1899–1902	Handled Britain's war effort in Boer War with South Africa
1902	Remained Colonial Secretary in new, Balfour-led Conservative government
1903	Resigned to campaign for tariff reform – the introduction of import duties on foreign goods; his campaign divided and damaged Conservatives, as he had divided Liberals
1906	Became seriously ill shortly after Conservative election catastrophe

Cold, chilling manner, single-minded, could be brash and pushy, often provocative in speech.

Aroused strong feelings of admiration and animosity.

Lord Salisbury on Chamberlain in 1884:

A Sicilian bandit.

A.J.P. Taylor[8] on Chamberlain:

Chamberlain's great energies and gifts were successful only in destruction ... He was unscrupulous in his means ... [He] brought a new bitterness into British politics. He was unsparing in victory, and savage in defeat

Peter Fraser[9] on Chamberlain:

It is not his theories or policies but his style and method which have proved of most lasting significance.

tax, local government reform and free elementary education. The vehemence of his attacks on those who opposed his approach roused them to fury. He portrayed Lord Hartington and the Whigs as a barrier to achieving his social aims. On the other side, Lord Salisbury and the Conservatives were denounced for their selfish defence of their class interests, 'the class who toil not, neither do they spin'. For many within both parties Chamberlain was too inflammatory, his language going 'too far'. They saw him as a demagogue promoting class warfare.

The publication of Gladstone's Home Rule Bill in 1886 provoked Chamberlain's opposition to official Liberal policy, and he and Hartington now found themselves fighting on the same side. However, they were temporarily consigned to the political sidelines, particularly after the failure of the Round-Table talks in 1887 which were designed to bring about a Liberal reunion.

By an irony of history Chamberlain now became drawn to the Conservative Party which he had spent his life denouncing. He was to spend the next 20 years of his stormy career in close co-operation with its leaders. Perhaps this was not totally surprising because in the mid-1870s he had found that he could work well with some of the Conservative ministers, particularly Cross, and he became convinced that Conservative philosophy could accommodate his social reforming views more easily than the Liberalism of Gladstone. Moreover, he began to develop close personal contacts with Conservatives, and found some of them both likeable and good company. In the cause of Empire he discovered an outlet for his ambitions which could be married to their preoccupations. His involvement with the Conservative Front Bench, especially Balfour, steadily developed after 1886, and Salisbury was willing to keep the Liberal Unionists informed of his government's intentions, and was ready to listen to their proposals.

By 1889 he was sharing a platform with Lord Salisbury, and found that he could work with him because the question of Ireland was overriding, far more important than any other issue. Chamberlain never completely abandoned his radicalism, and his commitment to social reform was the inspiration of his attitude to the Empire and Tariff Reform for he felt that the benefits of Empire might help to fund the advances in living conditions which he wished to see. Inevitably, opportunities within the Conservative Party for him to achieve this goal were slim. Yet his judicious combination of Empire and Social Reform did much to help him retain the loyalty of the working class in Birmingham, and it was his considerable achievement that he could carry the people of Birmingham with him despite his defection to the Conservative cause. The Chamberlains continued to dominate local politics until the end of our period.

A Note on ... Conservative fortunes, 1885–1906

For the 20 years after 1885, the Conservatives were to have a virtual monopoly of office. They won three out of the four elections, before they were soundly beaten in 1906. The Liberal Opposition was condemned to 18 years of parliamentary impotence and internal conflict.

Why did the Conservatives fare so well at this time?

The two decades of Conservative majorities had much to do with the impact of the Irish Question, for it was the issue of Home Rule for Ireland which inflicted such heavy damage on the Liberals' fortunes. The policy lacked attraction for English voters and provoked the break-up of the Gladstonian Party. Liberals such as Joseph Chamberlain and Lord Hartington seceded from their former party and Liberal Unionists increasingly came to be identified with the Conservatives. The coalition of conservative forces opposed to Home Rule (the Conservatives and Liberal breakaways) became known as the Unionists, although a formal merger did not come about until the organisational reforms of 1911, when the name 'Conservative and Unionist Party' was adopted.

For many people Ireland was the issue which transcended all others in importance. It was primarily the reason why a convinced Radical like Chamberlain could find himself on the same side of the political fence as the aristocratic Lord Salisbury, whom he had formerly so vehemently denounced. To Chamberlain, the new division in politics was clear:

1   I am, and shall be in the future, proud to call myself a Unionist, and be satisfied with that title alone, believing it is a wider and nobler title than either of Conservative or Liberal, since it includes them both – since it includes all men who are determined to maintain an
5   undivided Empire, and who are ready to promote the welfare and the union not of one class but of all classes of the community.

There were other factors at work. Gladstone's alleged radicalism, not just over Home Rule, had frightened some of the middle classes into joining with their opponents, for the Conservatives seemed to offer a sturdier defence of the rights of property. Peel had dreamed of a situation in which the Party would become the natural home for men of property, whatever the sources of their wealth, be it financial, industrial or landed. This at last seemed to be happening and it was Peel's disciple Gladstone who was helping to bring it about. As Salisbury remarked near to the close of his career: '[Gladstone's] existence was the greatest source of strength which the Conservative Party possessed'.

This powerful reinforcement added to Conservative wealth,

and the Conservative Party became adept at using its funds to reduce the opposition vote in elections. Voters still had to be registered, and sympathetic barristers were skilled at finding reasons for denying the franchise to likely opponents. The Conservatives could also afford to develop an organisation which maximised the Unionist vote now that the vast majority of men qualified.

An effort was made through the Primrose League to arouse wider public interest, and in inspiring leaflets such as *What the Conservatives have done for the British People*, much emphasis was placed on Conservative social reforms said to have been good for workingmen. The record of Disraeli seemed to add some weight to the claim, the more so as the Liberals had not been active in this area. It was an achievement of the Conservatives that they were able to make the party a home for the growing band of white-collar workers, be they professional or clerical. The League appealed both to those members of the middle and lower-middle classes who felt at home with the values of individual freedom, maintenance of the law, social betterment and imperial pride and to patriotic working men. It did valuable work in canvassing for their support and spreading the party message. Although Salisbury did little to promote the form of popular Conservatism which it represented, his leadership benefited substantially from its activities. It helped to create popular attachment to the Conservative Party, acting as what Martin Pugh[10] has called 'the vital bridge between parliamentary leaders and the mass electorate'.

Divisions among the party's opponents were of major importance. A weak and divided opposition has often been good for the right-wing cause in British politics, and the Liberals were seriously split after 1886. On issues other than Home Rule, different tendencies appeared in a party which still embraced coal owners as well as coal miners, factory owners as well as factory operatives. Many Liberals had their own 'fads'. For some, it was temperance (abstinence from strong drink), for others, it was Welsh Disestablishment (the ending in Wales of the special status of the Church of England). There were Liberal Imperialists and those like Lloyd George who were strongly opposed to imperial expansion. When the Boer War broke out in 1899 it exacerbated these divisions. A year later Lord Salisbury seized the initiative to call the Khaki election in which the Unionists exploited the patriotism of working men, and won handsomely.

Yet if the election of 1900 was the peak of Unionist electoral achievement, the war which made it possible sowed the seeds of Conservative decline. The length of time it took to subdue the Boers dented the mood of euphoria over Empire, and did much to reduce patriotic fervour. Chamberlain's policy of Tariff

Reform which aimed to bind the countries of the Empire together, was to prove even more damaging to the Unionists, and in the early years of the twentieth century it was their turn to split. As Peel had once divided them over the Corn Laws, so it was Chamberlain who did so over Protection. In so doing, he contributed significantly to Conservative difficulties and Liberal resurgence. In 1906 the Conservatives were reduced to a rump of 132 MPs, supported by 25 Liberal Unionists.

Neal Blewitt[11] has argued that Conservative success in the elections from 1886 to 1901 was built on fragile foundations. The victories resulted more from the problems of the Liberals in mobilising their potential supporters (especially because of Home Rule and the Boer War) than from positive endorsement of Conservative policies. The conditions were especially favourable for Unionists, but they were always liable to face a stronger challenge should the Liberals successfully regroup. In this context, the defeat faced by Balfour in 1906 is all the more understandable, because his government had not avoided mistakes and several of its policies only succeeded in uniting its Liberal enemies.

Richard Shannon[12] has also emphasised that Conservative predominance owed more to the problems of the party's opponents than to the careful planning of ministers. He quotes Salisbury's remark in 1882 and uses it as a text to assist in interpreting the period: 'Let us hope the chapter of accidents may help us: we shall hardly do much to help ourselves'. Shannon points out that Salisbury tended to react to events, his approach resting not on any purposeful plan but more on a process of adaptation to unforeseen circumstances. The key to his party's predominance was the opportunity to forge an alliance between the Conservatives and Liberal Unionists. But, Shannon argues, one of the side effects of this alliance was to stifle the emergence of new elements in the Party at large, so that it was ill adapted to meet the social challenges of the early twentieth century.

2 The Three Salisbury Administrations

> **KEY ISSUES** Why was Lord Randolph Churchill so dissatisfied with the performance of the Conservatives in office? What were the main domestic achievements of the Salisbury years?

a) Home Affairs: The Politics of 1885–6

On the fall of Gladstone's second administration in June 1885 Lord Salisbury agreed to form a minority government. He was at first reluctant for he knew that his position would be perilous with a few months to run in a 'hostile but dying' session of parliament. Nevertheless, with his backbenchers keen for office, he formed what Chamberlain disparagingly called 'the Ministry of Caretakers'. Little of significance occurred, other than the efforts of Lord Carnarvon, the new Viceroy of Ireland, to do a deal with Parnell. Carnarvon favoured a conciliatory approach to Irish problems, and was willing to offer some form of limited self-government. Churchill also wanted a generous settlement, although like Salisbury he was opposed to Home Rule. However, enough progress in the talks was made to convince Parnell that he could extract more from the Conservatives than from the Liberals. This led him to advise Irish voters in England to vote for Conservative candidates in the November general election. The outcome of polling was a deadlock, in which the 86 Parnellites held the balance. They kept the Conservatives in office, and Salisbury remained as Prime Minister.

Events took a dramatic turn when it became known in mid-December that Gladstone was in favour of Home Rule. His son, Herbert, revealed this information to the press, and alignments on the issue soon became clear-cut. In Salisbury's words, what had been a chimera now became a blazing issue. The Liberals became identified with Home Rule, although among prominent members of the party Chamberlain and Hartington were clearly hostile. The Conservatives viewed the prospect of Liberal disunity with glee. They came out in opposition, and Churchill began to exploit the Ulster question. He knew that the Protestants of the northern counties would never put up with becoming a minority in a predominantly Catholic Irish parliament.

As for Parnell, it became clear that he had miscalculated. It was now apparent that it was the Liberals, not the Conservatives, who were willing to recognise the aspirations of Irish people to govern themselves. His supporters combined with the Liberal opposition to bring down the Salisbury government in January 1886, and Gladstone again became Prime Minister. His intention was to produce a Home Rule Bill and, although Chamberlain joined the new government, he resigned when the details of the Bill became known to the Cabinet.

Chamberlain led the opposition in the House of Commons. He saw the measure as being 'tantamount to the break-up of the United Kingdom', for he believed that Home Rule would lead to independence. Conservatives shared his fears, and one of their pamphlets denounced Home Rule as a 'direct attack upon England and the English race'. Churchill was in the forefront of their attack. He warned that the Protestant Ulstermen of the northern counties would not accept domination by the Catholics who would outnumber them in an Irish parliament, saying 'Ulster will fight, and Ulster will be right'.

The Bill was defeated in the House of Commons by 30 votes as a result of the revolt by 93 dissident Liberals, including Hartington and

Chamberlain, who were known as Liberal Unionists. Their decision to vote against the Bill and bring down the government was made easier by the Conservative pledge not to oppose in the next election any Liberal MP who rebelled against the Gladstonian leadership. At this stage, there seemed little enthusiasm for any formal alliance between the two sides, and in the election which followed the government's defeat they fought separate campaigns. The Liberal Unionists, with 78 seats, held the balance in the new House, and generally gave their backing to what was an exclusively Conservative administration in its composition.

b) Salisbury's Second Administration, 1886–92: the Churchill–Salisbury clash

The early months of Lord Salisbury's government were dominated by the clash between Lord Randolph Churchill and the Prime Minister. Churchill had served in the brief ministry of 1885. As the Secretary of State for India he had shown an impressive mastery of detail and a capacity for hard work. Because of his performance and reputation he was an obvious candidate for high office when the Conservatives came back into office. He was appointed as Chancellor of the Exchequer, the youngest since Pitt, a post he combined with that of Leader of the House of Commons. From the beginning he proved to be a difficult colleague to work with as he was so unwilling to compromise.

It was inevitable that the views of the leader and those of Churchill should prove to be a cause of disharmony, for Churchill favoured a more vigorous approach to reform. He did not want the state merely to tinker with the established order of things. However, for a while, Salisbury hoped that his colleague was, underneath the veneer of a radical platform orator, at heart a traditional Conservative, and he treated him with some indulgence. Churchill was impatient for change, and the gulf between the two men widened. The Prime Minister was clearly irritated by the difficulties he encountered because of his ambitious colleague, and explained his tactics in a letter to Lord Cranbrook who had expressed his dismay at the way in which Salisbury was leaning over backwards to accommodate the Chancellor's feelings.

1 What you call my self-renunciation is merely an effort to deal with an abnormal and very difficult state of things. It arises from the peculiarities of Churchill ... [he] is the only possible leader in the House of Commons – and his ability is unquestionable. But he is wholly out of
5 sympathy with the rest of the Cabinet ... Like you, I am penetrated with a sense of the danger which the collapse of the Government would bring about; otherwise I should not have undertaken ... the task of leading an orchestra in which the first fiddle plays one tune and everybody else, including myself, wishes to play another.

The difficulties were political as well as personal, for they represented a divergent view of the nature of Toryism in a democratic age. Salisbury urged caution and wanted to keep the party together. Churchill felt frustrated, and in his Dartford Speech had proposed bold measures which he thought the party should take up. By early November 1886 Churchill's wayward, maverick personality and behaviour were wearying Salisbury, while Churchill was disillusioned that his Dartford programme was in danger of 'falling to pieces'. He believed that the Tories were proving 'incapable of reform', and he wrote to the Prime Minister to express his dismay:

1 I am afraid it is an idle schoolboy's dream to suppose that Tories can
   legislate – as I did – stupidly. They can govern and make wars, and
   increase taxation and expenditure a merveille, but legislation is not their
   province in a democratic constitution ... I certainly have not the
5 courage to go on struggling against cliques as poor Dizzy did all his life.

Salisbury's response is indicative of a very different approach. He believed in 'the art of the possible', and tried to emphasise this slower, more cautious and sceptical view of the nature of political change. His comments also reveal an acute and intuitive insight into the workings of the Conservative Party, as is revealed in his explanation of how the vested interests and classes powerful within the party would react to the attempt to force 'drastic, symmetrical measures' upon them:

1 The Tory Party is composed of varying elements, and there is merely
   trouble and vexation of spirit in trying to make them work together. I
   think the 'classes and dependents of class' are the strongest ingredients
   in our composition, but we have so to conduct our legislation that we
5 shall give some satisfaction to both classes and masses. This is specially
   difficult with the classes – because all legislation is rather unwelcome to
   them, as tending to disturb a state of things with which they are satisfied. It is evident, therefore, that we must work at less speed and at a
   lower temperature than our opponents. Our Bills must be tentative and
10 cautious, not sweeping and dramatic.

Soon afterwards Churchill ceased to be a problem. He presented the Cabinet with his Budget proposals, involving increases in death duties and cuts in military expenditure, in order to bring about reductions in personal taxation. The rest of his colleagues were unimpressed, and would not accept his plans. In particular, W.H. Smith, the Secretary for War, was irritated at both Churchill's manner and demands. He wrote to Salisbury:

1 It comes to this – is he to be the Government? If you are willing that
   he should be, I shall be delighted, but I could not go on, on such conditions. He is profoundly impressed with the belief that he has gauged
   the feeling of the Country and that he is right and everybody else is
5 wrong.

Churchill took the problem to the Prime Minister, demanding his support. Salisbury responded effectively. In such situations, he often retired to Hatfield to give himself time to think and manoeuvre. He preferred to fight his opponents from a distance and on this occasion he wrote to Churchill offering to put the matter of the military cuts to the Cabinet. It was not enough for the Chancellor, who impulsively resigned. Much to his fury, the resignation was unanswered for two days, whilst Salisbury checked that he had broad cabinet support. Then, with appropriate expressions of deep regret, he accepted the resignation – in Churchill's words, 'like a dog at a bone' – and replaced him as Chancellor with Goschen, a Liberal Unionist. This was to be the end of Churchill's ministerial career, and he was shortly struck down with a debilitating disease – probably a venereal one which he had contracted earlier in his colourful life. He devoted more and more time to the turf, and in the House his rare speeches were increasingly difficult to comprehend. He died in 1895.

Why did Churchill resign without putting up more of a fight? Perhaps he expected that his resignation would lead to the break-up of the government, or that it would be followed by his reinstatement, amidst popular acclaim. If this was the case, like many people, he overestimated his own importance. He was not indispensable and, although he had received popular backing in 1884, this time his support ebbed away with pathetic rapidity. There was always someone else. In his own words, 'I forgot Goschen'.

Then again, perhaps he had had enough. He was out of sympathy with the style and approach of most other ministers, and was a rather solitary figure in the party. Many Conservatives and Liberals regarded him as the 'incarnation of evil, a reckless and insolent iconoclast ... unscrupulous, violent, unprincipled ... one who, to serve the personal ambition which was his sole motive, would stick at nothing'. These were the words of Rosebery (later, a Liberal Prime Minister) who watched his performance from the other side of the House. If the judgement is rather too severe and unbalanced, it highlights the way in which many contemporaries thought of him. Having so little parliamentary or Cabinet support, perhaps the rejection of his proposals was just one rebuff too many. He knew that he and other ministers were in disagreement over many issues, and that, besides disputes on particular policies, there was a more general discord over the future direction of the party and the tempo of change.

If he did hope to survive his startling resignation, he chose the wrong time and the wrong issue. The timing was particularly poor, over Christmas when parliament was not in session. No one was likely to mobilise a campaign on his behalf amidst the seasonal festivities, as a skilful politician with sensitive antennae would surely have known. The issue was also not a crucial one, for economies could probably have been made in other departments, and did not have to come from the military, even though that was his clear preference.

As for Salisbury and the rest of the cabinet, they were relieved to see Churchill go. As Smith later wrote: 'the real truth is estimates are a pretext – not the real cause. It was really Salisbury or Churchill: and if Salisbury had gone, none of us could have remained'. Balfour could hardly believe how fortunate his uncle had been, noting how favourable the circumstances of resignation were for the Government:

1 He has not resigned as leader of the Tory Democrats'. He has resigned as a thwarted Ch. Of the Exchequer: – and not only that, but as a Ch. Of the Ex. thwarted on a point on which he will, I believe, carry with him none of the party. He has chosen his ground so badly that I am
5 almost tempted to think that he expects you to give way: – and yet he can hardly have so far lost his judgement!

ELEVENTH Year, No. 558.   THE DART.   Friday, July 8th, 1887.

THE PARTY OF TWO.

J. CHAMBERLAIN:—Yes, we can get on splendidly. I will be Premier, and you Chancellor———

LORD RANDOLPH:—Oh! No, pardon me. You must be Chancellor of the Exchequer and I, of course, will be Prem———

(Left deciding it.)

In 1887 both Chamberlain and Churchill were outside the party mainstream. Neither man was easily accommodated and both were ambitious. But whereas Chamberlain still had a political career ahead of him, Churchill was on the way down.

c) The Conservatives and Social Reform, 1886–92 and 1895–1902

Salisbury doubted whether anything useful could be achieved by state action in the field of social improvement, for he believed that the faults within society primarily arose from man's individual failings rather than some more generally treatable condition. Therefore, he had no wish to see his government pursue an actively reformist policy. He preferred instead to place the emphasis upon sound administration of the existing order. Nonetheless, his earlier fears about society had not yet been realised. The enlargement of the franchise had not produced mass anarchy, and though he was still anxious about 'dangerous' new forces such as socialism and the 'vast conflicts' which threatened the nation, he accepted that Conservatism need not be purely about resistance to improvement and the preservation of the status quo. Disraeli had endeavoured to make the Conservative Party one of national appeal, and limited change was acceptable if it furthered this end, whilst at the same time, did not threaten private property and individual rights.

Salisbury was, by preference, a believer in *laissez-faire*, but he felt some compassion for the poor and wished to ease their burdens a little. Such an approach made possible some limited and judicious reforms which would be beneficial to the lot of the working classes. He had, for instance, shown some interest in the problems of their housing in the early 1880s, and was later to legislate to remove some of its most unsatisfactory features in 1885 and 1890.

Most of those who believed in the Tory Democracy of Disraeli had passed from the scene by the mid 1880s, so that the era of improved trade-union rights, factory reform and advancements in public health was at an end. Those who took over the reins shared the Salisbury preference for 'good administration', for other than Churchill, in the early months, they were also concerned with issues such as militancy in the unions and the perils of any further movement towards democracy. They therefore also favoured cautious, worthwhile measures, which might bring some credit to the government's reputation. Sometimes the case for reform seemed to be a strong one, for a careful concession made at the right time could forestall a more sweeping measure from their opponents, when they next assumed office. Other causes were taken up when it was no longer easy to evade them.

The most effective reformer was C.T. Ritchie at the Local Government Board. He was a businessman, a minister rather in the mould of Sir Richard Cross. Like Cross, he proved to be a notable legislator, even if his reputation is rather less well-established. He was not a popular politician as Chamberlain and Churchill were, but in a quiet, workmanlike way he sponsored measures in whichever department he was placed. He was responsible for the Local Government (County Councils) Act of 1888. Salisbury anticipated that a Liberal government would ultimately adopt a more radical measure than anything he was prepared to contemplate. Because of this, he set aside his own preference for a cheaper system of indirect elections, and agreed to the scheme that Chamberlain was urging and which Ritchie also favoured. This set aside the rule of the Justices of the Peace, and replaced it with government by 62 directly-elected county councils, elected by the ratepayers. Towns of over 50,000 qualified for County Borough status, which gave them the same powers within their boundaries as the counties were granted. In view of its size, London received County Council status, and in his later ministry (1895–1902), Salisbury presided over the creation of a second tier of 28 London boroughs in 1899.

The Education Act of 1891 was another measure which Chamberlain was urging on the government, with support from Balfour. It introduced free elementary education. Salisbury accepted that once the state had made education compulsory it was only fair that there should be no financial burden on parents. Otherwise, he was unsympathetic to matters of popular education, which removed the opportunity for children to be at work and provide cheaper labour for the manufacturers. The government did introduce the Technical Instruction Act of 1889 which allowed local authorities to levy a penny in the £ rate for the purposes of providing technical education. The provision of such a skill was seen as beneficial both to those who received it and to their employers.

There were other measures, though most were of limited importance. The Allotments Acts encouraged local authorities to make land available for rural labourers for allotments and small-holdings. The Tithes Act placed the responsibility for paying the unpopular tax on owners rather than occupiers of land, thereby ending a cause for some resentment. There were also measures dealing with the hours of workers in shops and factories.

In Salisbury's third administration (1896–1902) reforms were few. In 1896 ministers tried to pass an Education Bill and a measure on agricultural rating, but dropped them for the session in the face of opposition in the House and outside. The Education Act of the following year was a much more modest measure to increase the state grant to Voluntary Schools. This primarily meant assisting the Church of England and Catholic schools. A measure to allow for derating of agricultural property did pass in 1897, much to Salisbury's pleasure, but in that year the most important measure was the Workmen's Compensation Act, piloted through the House by Joseph Chamberlain. Workers in several industries who received an injury in the course of their employment could now claim compensation from their employers. To some Conservatives, this was 'revolutionary', but Salisbury was prepared to back Chamberlain, having in 1895 committed this government to a more active social policy 'to ameliorate the conditions of the people' and bring about an 'improvement of the daily life of struggling millions'.

Chamberlain would have liked to see the government introduce Old-Age Pensions to reduce pauperism among the elderly. The Germans had old-age pensions introduced, and there was growing support in Britain for similar legislation. Chamberlain was the first leading politician to produce an actual scheme, and it may be that but for the outbreak of the Boer War something could have been achieved. Salisbury approved in principle a contributory scheme in which the state could establish the machinery, but not be faced with a serious financial burden. Once war broke out, such reforming proposals were shelved.

The legislative achievement of the Salisbury years was modest, although not without value. Certainly there was no spate of bold reforms, but this was only to be expected. After Disraeli's death the party was content with steady government, and accepted that the first task of ministers was to maintain the existing order. Salisbury's Conservatism was primarily defensive in character, concerned with protecting individual liberty and property, and this was what many of his party wanted. Improvements cost money, and the backbenchers were unhappy at the prospect of higher taxation or excessive burdens being placed on the rates. They welcomed the sort of policy which Salisbury had put to the voters in the 1892 election campaign. It promised to keep costs down. Little mention was made of social reform, and the emphasis was more upon the ability of the party to provide administration of superior competence to the Liberals.

Overall, the Salisbury approach made for what was once described as 'hesitant benevolence', doing good where this was not threatening to the individuals who hoped the Conservatives would look after them. Such an approach offered little to the working man in the towns, who might have preferred greater recognition of his rights, but the agricultural worker was less neglected. This was because this class had been given the vote in 1884, and both parties were looking for ways to attract the support of agricultural labourers, just as they had sought to do for the urban working man in the years of 1868–80. Moreover, in the 'Great Depression' of the 1880s, there was an obvious need to seek to relieve the lot of those who suffered from its worst effects, and in parts of the countryside its impact was serious.

Social reform in the period 1886–1902 generally reflected the views of the Conservative Prime Minister. Salisbury did not like the idea of 'programmatic politics', the notion that there was a series of commitments to be honoured. Individual measures were taken because they were desirable in themselves, given the condition of the country.

d) The Conservatives and Ireland

For the Conservatives, supported by the Liberal Unionists, the answer to Irish problems was a combination of stern government and modest reform. The policy was applied by the new Irish Secretary, Salisbury's nephew, Arthur Balfour, who was resolute in his determination to enforce the law. He believed that 'twenty years of firm government' were needed, and eventually he did succeed in restoring a fair measure of order. When agrarian disorders arose, his response was unwavering, and a demonstration at Mitchelstown, County Cork, was met by police fire resulting in several deaths. 'Remember Mitchelstown' was the Irish cry, and Balfour gained the nickname, 'Bloody Balfour', as a result of the brutal repression.

The policy was accompanied by one of moderate reform, for, although Balfour was determined to maintain the status quo in constitutional terms, he was ready to make concessions in an attempt 'to kill Home Rule by kindness'. In the short ministry of 1885, the Conservatives had passed the Ashbourne Act to make loans available for land purchase, and this was extended by Balfour. His 1891 Land Act established a Board to make funds available to those peasants who owned farms which were too small to be farmed economically. The measure was meant to encourage them to increase the size of their holdings, and it also made cheap seed and advice easily available to them.

As far as it went, it was a useful policy offering solid economic advantages, but the long history of neglect and hatred which soured relations between Britain and Ireland could not be overcome by such concessions, however well meant they were. The Catholics of Ireland regarded themselves as a nation who could govern themselves better than the British could. They were looking for the chance to do so and Home Rule was the only concession in which they were really interested.

Chamberlain had left the Liberal government to lead the opposition to the Home Rule Bill. In 1893 he was again the foremost opponent when Gladstone made a second attempt to introduce Home Rule. In the House of Lords, Hartington proposed its rejection and Salisbury spoke up for the Union of Britain and Ireland. The Bill was defeated.

e) Salisbury and Overseas Policy

In the late nineteenth century there were limits beyond which Lord Salisbury's governments would not go in pandering to the desires of the expanded electorate. But if it did not offer jam in the form of social legislation, at least it offered treacle in the form of a sentimental emotional approach to Empire. It was not so much a policy as a way of looking at the world. It emphasised the unrivalled prestige and might of the British Empire, and the force for good that Britain was in the world. It reflected a popular emotion, which made many people feel pride in the fact that God had accorded the British people the privilege of presiding over a quarter of the world, and assuming what the writer Kipling saw as the 'white man's burden'.

The Empire had been one of Disraeli's preoccupations in his Crystal Palace speech, and in the last decades of the century its greatest political exponent was Joseph Chamberlain, the Colonial Secretary after 1895. When he went over to the Conservative side he was able to offer the party the chance to share in his dream, 'to organise an Empire – one may almost say to create an Empire – greater and more potent for peace than any that history has yet known; that is a dream if you like, but a dream of which no man need be ashamed'.

Lord Salisbury was a more cautious imperialist, and was less romantic in his notions. He developed a mastery of the problems involved in the largely peaceful opening up of Africa, and his proven method of firm and patient negotiation suited the situation. He favoured a policy of colonial expansion and believed that it brought benefits both to Britain and to the territories that were added to the Empire. But he preferred commercial penetration to the military conquests of other nations, such as the French. He saw British influence as a 'great civilising Christianising force', with Britain being the territorial guardian under whom native peoples could develop in their own ways. Chamberlain felt similarly, although his speeches placed more emphasis upon the economic benefits of Empire. He was a colonial reformer and also favoured schemes of imperial federation, especially for defence purposes. However, little was achieved in either of these directions, mainly because the policies were inhibited by a lack of Treasury funds, and the Empire developed as a partnership without formal ties.

Imperialism suffered a major setback in the Boer War (1899–1902), which was the culmination of prolonged friction between the British and the Boers in southern Africa. The Boer farmers in the independent republics of the Transvaal and the Orange Free State felt threatened by the British immigrants, whom they called 'Uitlanders', who were flooding into their countries in search of gold and diamonds, and who threatened to outnumber them in the foreseeable future, whilst the settlers felt that their basic rights were being denied. Joseph Chamberlain was widely seen by his critics as a 'warmonger' whose speeches and actions had been provocatively anti-Boer. On neither side was there a spirit of compromise, and war followed.

The Boers gained several initial successes, for they had the advantage of knowing their country well. It required heavy reinforcements in 1900 to turn the tide, and though the British emerged victorious, it was only after the Boers had staged a two-year display of effective guerilla warfare. Moreover, in order to win the war, it was seen as necessary to confine the Boer population in special reserves, the first 'concentration camps', and the barbaric methods involved in the fighting, as well as the difficulty in overcoming the Boers, did much to discredit the cause of Imperialism.

Salisbury had had doubts about the conduct of events leading to the war, and disliked its necessity. In overseas matters, his approach was one of peaceful negotiation where possible, and he was noted for his coolness in international disputes – his 'masterly inactivity'. As he put it, 'British policy is to drift lazily down stream, occasionally putting out a boathook to avoid a collision'. He was prepared to 'put out a boathook' if he perceived that, without some initiative, a situation could damage British interests. He was particularly critical of Gladstone's policies between 1880 and 1885 which, he felt, had left the country exposed and alone, and he accused the Liberals of 'uniting the Continent of Europe – against England'. He used the term 'splendid isolation' in discussing his policy, and though he meant it to be a warning about the situation in which Britain might find itself, it has often inaccurately been used to describe his outlook.

In the period up to 1890, he was faced by Bismarck's diplomatic skills. Bismarck was increasing the size of the German army and signed a Reinsurance Treaty with Russia in 1887. Salisbury was worried about Russian designs in the Balkans, and a possible threat to the security of the Mediterranean. Therefore, he concluded two Mediterranean Agreements, with Italy and then with Austria, which were vague promises of mutual support. These were aimed primarily at Russia which, along with France, was seen as a potential enemy. Germany was not viewed as a likely foe. In fact, Germany was keen to conclude an alliance with Britain in 1889, shortly before Bismarck's fall. Salisbury remained wary of formal alliances, of the kind that other powers were fond of making. He saw them as commitments which could entangle Britain in disputes not of primary concern. However, aware of the growing closeness of the Franco-Russian axis, and of the weakness of British sea-power, his Government passed a Naval Defence Act in 1899 to increase the size and quality of the navy.

The generally peaceful partitioning of the African continent, the skilful resolution of international disputes and the establishment of a strong navy were to his credit, and his period at the helm was one of British strength and power, 'the high tide of British imperialism and power in the world'. The celebration of the Golden and Diamond Jubilees of Queen Victoria in 1887 and 1897 had provided a chance for the nation to bask in national and imperial pride, confident of its place in the world. That confidence was to be dented seriously by the failures of the Boer War. Until then, however, Salisbury's achievements on the global scene were impressive, and as Winston Churchill[13] put it, 'no Foreign Secretary has ever wielded the diplomatic boathook with greater dexterity'.

f) Salisbury's Resignation

At the turn of the century the Conservatives seemed secure. The Khaki Election of 1900 was successfully fought, the Liberals were divided over the war, and there seemed no reason for the long period of

Conservative dominance to come to an end. Salisbury stepped down from the premiership in 1902, and the succession was well-timed. He hoped to ease his nephew, Arthur Balfour, into the leadership, and at the time Chamberlain was briefly out of action, having been run over by a passing cab. In any case, although Chamberlain was a more dynamic contender, he was not a true Conservative. He was still a Liberal Unionist, a partner of the official party, but one which retained its separate identity until the reforms of 1911. Many Conservatives would have felt unhappy with an ex-Radical at their head.

3 The Premiership of Balfour

> **KEY ISSUES** What qualities did Arthur Balfour bring to the Premiership? To what extent must he bear the primary responsibility for the party's defeat in the 1906 election?

Arthur Balfour had many gifts. He possessed a fine intellect and an ability to analyse any problem. He was an amateur philosopher, the author of *A Defence of Philosophical Doubt,* and was according to his contemporary, Lord Birkenhead, 'the finest brain that has been applied to politics in our time'. A bachelor of wit, elegance and charm, he was a welcome guest in any English country house where his social gifts went down well. Lloyd George captured something of his rather effeminate style in his dismissive remark that he was 'just like the scent on a pocket handkerchief'.

Balfour's wealth and background, his cultural preoccupations, and his languid air made him appealing to those of his own class. He was a 'Conservative's Conservative'. He had much less appeal to the 'man in the street', and showed little awareness of their feelings. As Joseph Chamberlain's eldest son, Austen, observed: 'He has no comprehension of the habits or thoughts of his countrymen, and no idea how things strike them'. He was unusually remote from the problems of everyday life. Neither was he particularly well-suited to the position of party leader. For all of his intellectual excellence and acknowledged ability, he was not to be a success. Within the Cabinet he took open-mindedness too far. It was commendable to see both sides of a question, but unfortunately he seemed unable ever to come down on one side and give a lead. He was open to the charge of indecision, and though he had a certain dexterity in improvisation and surviving scrapes, these were not qualities which inspired the party or the voters. Moreover, he was unsympathetic to the business interest, which was becoming more important in the party.

The 'social question' did not occupy a high place in his thoughts, and unlike Chamberlain he had no great desire to get things done. He could see the problems which demanded attention, but he did not look too hard for solutions to them. He shared his uncle's general distrust of political and economic change. Although he was keen to credit the Conservatives with most of the important reforms of the nineteenth century, he was not the man to embark on many new ones. In tackling any social issue, he stressed the importance of ensuring that individual effort was not discouraged, for he believed that the self-reliance of people who used their talents to the full was the best means of raising the general standard. Neither did he think that one class should benefit from confiscation from another, and he was reluctant to see reform paid for by burdens on his own class. As he later put it, when opposing the Liberal Chancellor of the Exchequer, '... not out of the kind of taxes put on by Lloyd George'.

At the time of his takeover the situation looked promising, because he had an overall parliamentary majority and faced a divided and weak opposition. He soon showed unusual tenacity in pushing a controversial Education Bill through the House of Commons. This abolished the School Boards established by the Liberals in 1870 and put elementary education into the hands of elected local councils. It also encouraged Local Education Authorities to 'survey the needs of their area' for secondary education, and enabled them to make technical and even adult provision. The 'Balfour Act' was a landmark in the history of English education, for it not only brought about unified control but for the first time dealt with elementary and higher education together. It was a considerable personal achievement for Morant, the civil servant who largely drafted the Bill, and Balfour, who gave him his whole-hearted backing, and it provided the basic idea for the local administration of education for over 40 years. Yet commendable though the initiative was, Balfour showed insensitivity in his handling of the religious issues which dogged any reform in this area, and antagonised the Nonconformists by offering rate-aid to Church of England schools; in Wales particularly, the Nonconformists kept up strong resistance. They had looked forward to the impending bankruptcy of this sector, and Balfour's measure was to give Church schools new life.

He achieved little else in the social field, other than the Unemployed Workmen Act of 1905, which established Distress Committees in the larger towns to help the unemployed to find work. These Committees were empowered, among other things, to open labour exchanges and to aid emigration, and the ideas the Act represented were in some respects useful. However, they had nothing to offer for many of the unemployed. For many who were suffering hardship, the last resort remained the hated workhouse system created by the New Poor Law of 1834.

In particular, Balfour was unwilling to address the issues created by a series of legal judgments which cast doubt upon the position in law of the Trade Unions. Disraeli had been happy to restore rights to working men; Balfour offered them little, at a time when workers were anxious about their legal position and right to strike. A decision in the Taff Vale case, upheld by the House of Lords in 1901, had made it clear that a union's funds were liable for civil damages. In other words, unions might have to pay for damages (costs and inconvenience) suffered by an employer because of strike action.

Balfour was similarly insensitive in his reaction to the introduction of Chinese labour into South Africa, a policy which was denounced at the time as 'Chinese slavery'. It was upsetting to the nonconformist conscience and it offended British workers on economic and humanitarian grounds. Conditions of work there were an affront to liberal and humane people, whilst trade unionists and others particularly dwelt on the terms of pay and employment; some resented the loss of employment opportunities to British workers.

Balfour was more successful in matters of foreign policy and defence. The Anglo-Japanese Treaty of 1902, the creation of the Committee of Imperial Defence, and the introduction of reforms in the army and navy were useful achievements. Moreover, the Land Purchase Act introduced by George Wyndham in 1903 was a beneficial continuation of the Conservative policy of 'killing Home Rule by kindness', and did much finally to resolve the land question in Ireland by enabling many tenants to become peasant proprietors as a result of long-term loans at low rates of interest. However, the issue which dominated his administration and seriously split the Conservative Party was that of tariff reform.

a) The Tariff Reform Controversy

Joseph Chamberlain, still at the Colonial Office, had a vision of imperial strength based on some kind of a federal structure, underpinned by military unity and a customs union. Over the former he was thwarted by other statesmen at the Colonial Conference of 1902 which he chaired. But in 1903 he put forward a bold scheme for tariff reform which in reality meant a return to protectionism. Disraeli, the earlier Tory advocate of protection, had been converted to free trade and this policy had been the accepted orthodoxy in both parties ever since. Now Chamberlain was talking of retaliatory tariffs against those countries which applied duties against British goods, and of imperial preference, a policy by which Britain and the dominions gave each other preferential rates of duties so that Commonwealth trade was promoted at the expense of trade with other countries.

In so doing, Chamberlain took up an issue which was not to be resolved within the party for another three decades. It was an issue which never provided the Conservatives with any electoral advantage, and on occasion did them much harm. The immediate impact of his move was to rally the disunited Liberals and open a serious breach in the Conservative Party. Some government supporters, such as the old Whig, Lord Hartington, now the Duke of Devonshire, were in favour

HISTORY REVERSES ITSELF:

OR, PAPA JOSEPH TAKING MASTER ARTHUR A PROTECTION WALK.

PAPA JOSEPH. "COME ALONG, MASTER ARTHUR. *DO* STEP OUT!"
MASTER ARTHUR. "THAT'S ALL VERY WELL, BUT YOU KNOW I CANNOT GO AS FAST AS YOU DO."

Punch cartoon, 1903.
Joseph Chamberlain wanted to see positive leadership from Balfour, taking the party down the road marked 'Protection'. Balfour, aware of the difficulties within the party, was more hesitant.

of free trade. More, perhaps one third of the parliamentary party, were in agreement with Chamberlain, and many more were in the middle, like Balfour himself. He inclined to Chamberlain's view, but felt that the issue was better taken up after an election, for it was bound to damage party unity.

Balfour tried to hold the ring and keep his Cabinet and party together, but Chamberlain was not to be silenced. The result was that in September 1903 several ministers, including Chamberlain and Hartington, left the government. Chamberlain sought to rally the country in support of his new cause. He knew that he needed working-class support, but workers were suspicious of the benefits which he claimed for tariff reform. He argued that opening up colonial trade would provide greater employment opportunities in the Empire. He also said that if British firms were less exposed to competition, then home industry would flourish. From the prosperity so generated, the government would finance social reform. Workers had no reason to believe that a Unionist government under Balfour would offer much in the way of social reform, and there was no guarantee that the prospects of greater employment would come about. On the other hand, more expensive food would be a reality. Tariffs on imported corn would mean dearer bread, as Liberals reminded the electorate in posters depicting the large loaf they could have with Free Trade, and the smaller one under Chamberlain's scheme.

Balfour was in a difficult position. The Conservative cause was bitterly divided, and his attempt to placate all elements and keep the party together was understandable. But he was left looking indecisive. A contemporary ditty outlined his position:

I'm not for Free Trade, and I'm not for Protection
I approve of them both, and to both have objection.

b) The 1906 Election

In December 1905, Balfour had had enough and resigned. The incoming Liberal administration quickly called an election for January. This was to be disastrous for the Conservatives, yielding their lowest total of MPs for many years. The Liberals had an overwhelming majority over all parties, and they were likely to gain Irish and Labour support. To Balfour perhaps the most ominous portent in the election was the arrival of 53 Labour/Lib-Lab MPs – 'the cork bobbing on the socialist tide'.

Why were the Unionists so savaged at the polls?

Balfour's government had started with some advantages, but it also had what Winston Churchill described as 'an exhausted inheritance'. The Party had been long in office, and the 'time for a change' argument was a strong one. Moreover, the Liberals, united by various Unionist actions, now looked in better shape. The Education and Chinese Slavery issues had rallied the nonconformists to their side.

Party organisation had been allowed to run down (see page 150), and the creaking machine made it more difficult for them to maximise their vote in several parts of the country. Neither did the staggering of elections over three weeks help, for the early results in free-trade Lancashire registered a strong swing to the Liberals which voters elsewhere were aware of when they made their choice. There may have been a temptation for the uncommitted to jump on the winning bandwagon.

Two issues stand out. The dissension in the party over tariff reform created a seriously damaging image, and, in any case, the policy lacked public appeal. Yet perhaps more important was Tory neglect of the social question, for this election was the first since the last extension of the vote in which there was no distracting issue such as Home Rule or the Boer War. Working people had 'come of age', and were looking for improvements in their living and working conditions. Whereas the Liberals made some vague promises of social improvement, the Conservatives offered little and the failure to reverse the Taff Vale Judgement cost them dear.

Chamberlain is often blamed for the Unionist defeat, and there is no doubt that his insistence on taking up the tariff question was electorally harmful. He must take some of the blame for the failure to reverse the Taff Vale decision, for his reforming vision did not embrace the rights of trade unions. However, he had warned Balfour about the dangers the Education Act would cause, and, by then out of office, had opposed Chinese Slavery. He had also urged that the election be called earlier, and certainly the longer it was delayed the more damaging was the internal feuding.

Chamberlain had the satisfaction of seeing a majority of his supporters returned in the election, for it was established that there were 109 Chamberlainites, and only 16 'Free Fooders'. His own and other seats in Birmingham were held against the tide, as was his son's, in Worcester. The Chamberlains were keen party organisers, and never allowed their local machinery to atrophy as happened in other parts of the country. Even more satisfying, whilst he was handsomely re-elected, Balfour and some other Cabinet Ministers were defeated, and for a few weeks he led the party in opposition. If he had wanted to, he could probably have seized the leadership, but by 1906 he was too fatigued and had lost the appetite for battle. Soon afterwards, he had left the political scene after suffering a stroke.

c) The Tories in Opposition, 1905–14

The Liberals were in command of the House of Commons, but were vastly outnumbered in the House of Lords. Very soon, they ran into difficulty with their programme of legislation, and the key to their problem lay in a little-noticed speech of Balfour early in 1906. In it he made his intentions clear: 'The great Unionist Party should still control, whether in power or whether in opposition, the destinies of this great Empire'. He later told Landsdowne, the party leader in the Lords, that 'the two Houses shall not work as separate armies, but shall co-operate in a common plan of campaign ... The real discussion ... is not now in this House [of Commons] ... the real discussion must be elsewhere'.

The Conservatives regarded themselves as the natural rulers of the nation, and seemed intent on governing whether they were in or out of office. The party was in a negative frame of mind, and members did not make the necessary adjustment to their reduced influence. Their mood was aggressive, and many were not particularly choosy about the tactics it adopted. This period was one of the least attractive in party history, and even pro-Conservative writers have portrayed it as one in which the Conservatives lost their collective good sense. Racked by continuing dissension over Tariff Reform, they opposed most of the changes which the Liberals proposed – such as Old Age Pensions and National Insurance against sickness and unemployment, policies which they regarded as confiscation of property rights and a threat to any idea of individual responsibility.

Most of the Conservatives in the House of Lords rejected Lloyd George's radical Budget of 1909, which had been skilfully framed so that it would appear that by opposing it, the peers were acting in defence of their own privileges and interests. The outcome of the Lords' rejection was a Constitutional Crisis, involving two elections in 1910, in which the Conservatives improved their position and the Liberals lost their overall majority. They continued to govern only with Irish and Labour support. The result was that the Liberals produced a Parliament Bill in 1910 which sought to curtail the powers of the Upper House. Balfour accepted that the Budget must pass, and tried to be constructive in discussions with Asquith (the Liberal Prime Minister) over the powers of the House of Lords. Other Unionists were less willing to compromise, and became scornful of his more reasonable approach. They began to mutter 'BMG', Balfour Must Go. The days of the 'Hotel Cecil', as the Balfour-Salisbury family faction was known, were numbered.

d) Events in Ireland

Dependent on Irish support in the House of Commons, the Liberal government came under pressure to revive the issue of self-government for Ireland, the policy of Home Rule which had lain dormant since 1894. Now that the Lords had lost its permanent veto over legislation, the Liberals had no excuse for not making a third bid, and they drew up a Home Rule Bill in 1912. This provoked a second serious constitutional battle, for the Liberal Bill again made no separate provision for the Protestants of Ulster who feared that their interests would be overridden in a predominantly Catholic Irish parliament. As long ago as 1885 Lord Randolph Churchill had warned that 'Ulster will fight, and Ulster will be right'. His words came true, for now that there was no barrier to the passage of a Home Rule Bill, the fears of Ulstermen increased and they were determined to resist.

Balfour had resigned in November 1911 when it was clear that the whispering campaign against his leadership showed no sign of abating. His successor, Andrew Bonar Law, was a man of very different background and style. He was a shrewd businessman with a good head for statistics. He had developed a mastery of the details of Tariff Reform, of which he was in favour, and of the Ulster issue, on which he held firm, indeed unmovable, beliefs. He was strongly identified with the Ulster cause, at the very time when the situation there was becoming acute. He held his views sincerely, and with deadly earnest: 'These people are prepared to die for their convictions'. He sympathised with those convictions, for he had a Scottish Presbyterian background himself, and therefore shared a similar set of narrow Protestant beliefs.

When the Ulster Volunteers were formed to resist Home Rule, the Unionists gave them their backing. Bonar Law bluntly said that he could not imagine any 'length of resistance to which Ulster can go in which I should not be prepared to support them'. This was perilously close to supporting rebellion, and in so aligning himself with the extremists he was placing the Unionist Party, normally so proud of its reputation as the party of law and order, on the side of those who ignored the rule of law. He was echoing the mood of frustration in a party which had been defeated three times in four years at the polls, and which had ultimately been forced to swallow the Budget and the Parliament Bill. They could not stomach another climbdown. The beginning of the First World War saved the day in this respect at least for, although the Home Rule Bill became law, it was suspended for the duration of international hostilities, and an all-out constitutional crisis thus averted.

e) Women and the Vote

Edwardian politics were turbulent and the threat to parliamentary government was wide-ranging. However, unlike the crises over the Budget and Home Rule, the issue of women's rights was to cut across party lines.

Women were unable to vote in parliamentary elections, although they were allowed to in local government elections. They could serve on school boards after 1870; from 1907 they could sit on county and county borough councils. This degree of local involvement was accepted by many men because they thought that local politics directly affected women's domestic concerns by dealing with such issues as the education of their children. However, no progress had been made on 'votes for women' in parliamentary elections. John Stuart Mill had tried to get the female franchise written into the 1867 Bill but had not succeeded, and in the years afterwards the campaigning of the National Union of Women's Suffrage Association had not brought any reward. In 1903 the Women's Social and Political

Union began to attract public attention because of the militancy of its members who resorted to direct action to boost their cause. These Suffragettes, as they were known, expected politicians to declare themselves for or against women's right to vote. The issue provoked major disagreements within each of the parties.

Opinion among rank-and-file Conservatives was generally hostile to the women's cause and particularly to the methods of the WSPU. The leadership were generally more sympathetic. As long ago as 1848 Disraeli had referred to the 'justice of the women's cause' but in 1867, when piloting his Bill through the House, he offered personal sympathy, but would not commit his party to action. This was typical of subsequent behaviour. The Conservatives gave expressions of support while in opposition, but did nothing when the party was in office.

Lord Salisbury supported women's suffrage, believing that 'by knowledge, by training and by character, women had much to contribute, especially in the fields of morality and religion'. Balfour was more strongly sympathetic, and often spoke in favour in the House of Commons. Yet in the long period of almost uninterrupted Tory rule from 1885 to 1905 both of them were unwilling to press the issue because of backbencher opposition; ultimately, they did not consider it sufficiently important to merit action. Conservative leaders tended to see this as a distracting question, which would arouse much opposition within the party, without bringing tangible gains.

A Note on ... Party organisation
Lord Randolph Churchill realised the importance of ensuring that the party in London was in touch with the party in the country. He wanted to see Conservatism develop as a popular movement and argued for a bold approach to make it more democratic. It particularly concerned him that the leadership did not reflect the increasingly middle-class composition of many Associations. However, many leading Conservatives were uneasy at this change of character in party membership. They wished to cling to their positions. When Churchill was elected as Chairman of the National Union, and was in a position to challenge party control, he was involved in a behind-the-scenes struggle with the elements who wished to resist change, whom he described as 'the old men crooning over the fire at the Carlton Club'. At one point he resigned and was reinstated with acclaim, a precedent which did not recur when he resigned from the Salisbury government in 1886.

Ultimately he was more interested in policy than organisation, and before the 1885 election he made his peace with Salisbury. He ceased to promote internal party democracy in return for greater recognition of his talents within the leadership. The issue had given him a chance to raise his profile and to gain publicity, and he was content to drop it when it had served its purpose. Perhaps he was aware that if he reached the position of Leader, he might not appreciate any attempt by the mass of the party to be closely involved in policy formulation.

As it was, Salisbury placed reform of the party organisation in the capable hands of Richard Middleton and yielded nothing on the formation of party policy. The central machinery was to operate smoothly over the next 17 years, and its efficient functioning helped the party to win four of the five elections following Middleton's appointment. On his resignation in 1903, dissension was rife and the lack of harmony between those in charge aggravated Conservative problems in the run-up to the 1906 debacle.

a) The Party in the Country

Salisbury accepted the need for the party to respond to the extensions of the franchise in 1867 and 1884. He approved of the network of Conservative workingmen's clubs which was being created around the country, and came to see that a mass Conservative movement under the watchful eye of the party elders could prove most beneficial in mobilising support for the party.

In particular, Salisbury showed interest in another organisation with which Churchill had been involved, the Primrose League. The League was dedicated to upholding the Church, the Constitution and the traditional national virtues, as well as perpetuating the memory of its hero, Disraeli. In its early days it was much influenced by Churchill's personality and outlook, but it gradually developed its own distinctive ethos. It was generally loyal to the leadership and did much to arouse an interest in the party's affairs. It organised many social events, such as concerts and entertainments, and women played a significant role in them. Membership grew rapidly, especially in rural areas, and was fuelled by anti-Home Rule feeling and the new emphasis upon the imperial theme. The League soon developed widespread support around the country, bringing together people from different walks of life in an organisation which encouraged them to work with another for the good of the party.

Another vehicle for the expression of Conservative feeling was the Tariff Reform League through which Chamberlain tried to convert the country to the cause of protectionism and imperial preference. The movement received its initial impetus from the Birmingham Tariff Committee, in which local businessmen were prominent. A national body was rapidly established and soon the London headquarters was co-ordinating branches up and down the country. Mass rallies and smaller meetings were held, and the body exploited the new techniques of popular communication, using songs, records, plays and leaflets to get its message across.

b) The Organisational Reforms of 1911

Defeat is often a spur to organisational improvement, and following the electoral setbacks of 1910 Balfour appointed an enquiry into the whole structure of the Party. The outcome was an amalgamation of the Liberal Unionists and Conservatives, to give the party its modern title, the Conservative and Unionist Party. The relationship of each branch of the machinery to other ones was finally clarified, particularly that between Central Office and the National Union. The new office of Party Chairman was created, and he was to become the head of Central Office, which was given full control over organisation and publicity. The Chief Whip lost any wider organisational duties, and the National Union was to be an influential medium of two-way communication between the country and the leadership, but not a body exercising power.

References

1   R. Blake, *The Conservative Party from Peel to Major* (Heinemann, 1997)
2   Lady Gwendoline Cecil
3   R. Blake, *The Conservative Party from Peel to Major*
4   P. Marsh, *The Discipline of Popular Government: Lord Salisbury's Domestic Statecraft 1881–1902* (Harvester Press, 1978)
5   *Ibid.*
6   A. Roberts, *Salisbury: Victorian Titan* (Weidenfeld and Nicolson, 1999)
7   M. Bentley, *Politics Without Democracy 1915–1914* (Fontana, 1984)
8   A.J.P. Taylor, *Politics in Wartime and Other Essays* (Hamish Hamilton, 1964)
9   P. Fraser, *Joseph Chamberlain, Radicalism and Empire 1868–1914* (Cassell, 1966)
10 M. Pugh, *The Making of Modern British Politics 1867–1939* (Blackwell, 1982)
11 N. Blewitt, *The Peers, the Parties and the People: the General Elections of 1910* (Macmillan, 1972)
12 R. Shannon, *The Age of Salisbury 1881–1902* (Longman, 1996)
13 W. Churchill, *A History of the English Speaking Peoples* (Cassell, 1951, reissued 1999)

Summary
The Era of Salisbury and Balfour, 1881–1914

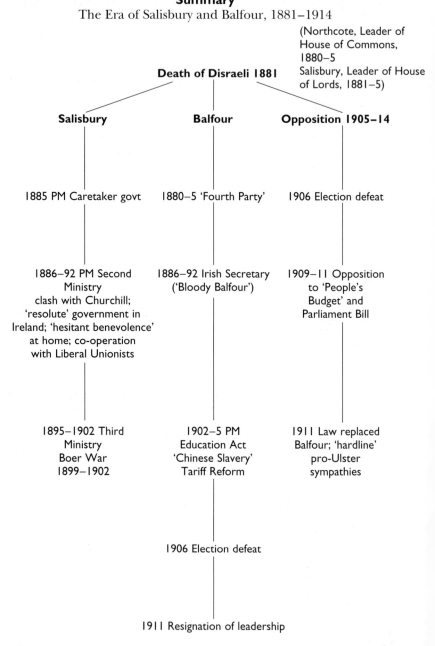

(Northcote, Leader of
House of Commons,
1880–5
Salisbury, Leader of House
of Lords, 1881–5)

Death of Disraeli 1881

Salisbury   **Balfour**   **Opposition 1905–14**

1885 PM Caretaker govt   1880–5 'Fourth Party'   1906 Election defeat

1886–92 PM Second
Ministry
clash with Churchill;
'resolute' government in
Ireland; 'hesitant benevolence'
at home; co-operation
with Liberal Unionists

1886–92 Irish Secretary
('Bloody Balfour')

1909–11 Opposition
to 'People's
Budget' and
Parliament Bill

1895–1902 Third
Ministry
Boer War
1899–1902

1902–5 PM
Education Act
'Chinese Slavery'
Tariff Reform

1911 Law replaced
Balfour; 'hardline'
pro-Ulster
sympathies

1906 Election defeat

1911 Resignation of leadership

Working on Chapter 5

You will need to make a brief set of notes about each of the four main characters – Lord Randolph Churchill, Joseph Chamberlain, Lord Salisbury and Arthur Balfour – discussed in this chapter. There should be three sections in each set of notes. The subheadings to use for these sections are: i) Personality and Character, ii) Approach to Politics/Policies, and iii) Strengths and Weaknesses as a Team Member.

Your second task is to construct a table showing the similarities and differences between the Disraelian and post-Disraelian Conservative parties. Brief comments entered in a two-column table will be sufficient.

Answering structured and essay questions on Chapter 5

Describe exactly what you are required to do in answering each part of the following structured question.

a) What were the achievements of the Conservative governments of the period 1886 to 1905?
b) Why was more not achieved?
c) Was the defeat of the Conservatives in the 1906 election their own fault? Explain your answer.

In which two parts of this question are you definitely expected to present different points of view? How could different points of view be built into an answer to the other part?

Essay questions on the Conservative Party in the age of Salisbury and Balfour often concentrate on the main characters in the political life of the period. You could well be asked to concentrate on similarities and differences. Examine the following questions:

1. Why did Lord Randolph Churchill find it impossible to work harmoniously with his Cabinet colleagues?
2. In what ways were the Liberal Unionists uncomfortable bedfellows with the Conservatives in the period 1886 to 1906?
3. What did the 'Hotel Cecil' and Joseph Chamberlain share in common?
4. 'Lord Salisbury, as Prime Minister, was out of touch with the popular feelings of the time.' Do you agree?

Only one of these questions requires you to present different points of view. Which one is it? In answers to 'on the one hand, yes, on the other hand, no' questions which part of your argument do you present first?

Source-based questions on Chapter 5

1. Salisbury as Prime Minister
Read the extracts on pages 131–2 and answer the following questions:

a) From the evidence of his letter to Cranbrook, why do you think that Salisbury tolerated the presence of Churchill in his government? (*3 marks*)

b) From extracts two and three explain how Salisbury's view of the purpose of government differs from that held by Churchill. (*4 marks*)

c) Using evidence from all of these extracts give reasons why Salisbury found Churchill to be such a difficult colleague. (*4 marks*)

d) Salisbury has been described as a pessimist by nature. What evidence can be found in these extracts to support that view? (*4 marks*)

e) From the evidence of these extracts and from your own knowledge, how highly do you rate Salisbury as a prime minister and as a party leader? (*10 marks*)

2. The Return of Protection
Study the cartoon on page 144 and note the contemporary ditty on page 145 and then answer the following questions:

a) In the context of politics in 1903 explain your understanding of the cartoon. (*3 marks*)

b) Why might a historian find evidence such as cartoons and trivial songs of value and yet wish to exercise caution in using their evidence? (*3 marks*)

c) What questions do the two pieces of evidence cited raise about Arthur Balfour as a political leader? (*4 marks*)

d) Why did the issue of tariff reform divide the Conservative party so deeply in the early years of the twentieth century? (*10 marks*)

6 Conclusion

POINTS TO CONSIDER

In the nineteenth century, the Conservative party successfully adapted to changing circumstances and because of this was able to appeal widely enough within the community to gain electoral success. It had dominated British politics for the two decades between 1885–1905 and though it was out of office in the years before World War One there was no doubt that it remained the alternative government.

As you read this chapter, you need to reflect upon the elements of change and continuity within the party. Ask yourself what the party stood for and be able to identify its main strengths and weaknesses in 1914. Think about which party, the Liberals or the Conservatives, was in the healthier state. Consider what sort of people were to be found within the Conservative ranks, both at Westminster and beyond, and on which groups the party primarily based its support?

1 Electoral Politics

KEY ISSUES Why had the Conservative party fared so well in nineteenth-century elections? In what respects did it seem to have lost its touch in the decade before 1914?

In 1815 the Tories began our period with a prolonged spell in government. In 1914 they were in opposition and in recent years had suffered three successive election defeats. Yet, despite its ailing fortunes in Edwardian Britain, the Party had generally done well in elections between 1815 and 1914. After a lean generation following the fall of Peel it had come to dominate the last three decades of the century. It had tasted the success of almost 50 years of single-party government and above all had survived into a more democratic age. That, in itself, was a tribute to their power of adaptation, for landed parties of the Right, dedicated to preserving the interests of privilege and property, largely fizzled out in continental Europe. In Britain not only did Conservatism survive, it also flourished. This was in spite of the fact that the vote was extended to working people who formed a majority of the electorate. Their class interests did not at first sight appear to coincide with those of the Conservatives.

The Unionist record in opposition after 1906 was not impressive. Much energy was wasted on the disagreements over tariff reform and on internal party manoeuvres. After 1911 the new leadership did spend more time harassing the government and this helped to hold the party together. But it was a unity based on negation, for little thought had gone into formulating a Conservative approach to the great issues of the day, particularly the social one. Many Unionists were hopeful of victory in the next election, whenever that might be, after the erosion of Liberal support in 1910 and in subsequent by-elections. However, of course, they could not be certain. In electoral terms they had recovered well, but they would still be dependent on Liberal mistakes and divisions and on the unpopularity of the government over the Ulster question to get them back into power. And the Liberals could not be under-estimated. Despite their problems they were resilient, and there were able men in their ranks whose resourcefulness was not to be doubted.

2 Party Support in 1914

> **KEY ISSUE** What were the sources of Conservative strength in 1914?

The Party had some things going very much in its favour. Although it was in a minority in the House of Commons, it remained in control of the House of Lords where there was a massive in-built Conservative majority. It is true that the second chamber had lost its permanent veto, but the Conservatives could still use it to delay any legislation of which they disapproved.

In the country, Unionist support was strong in certain areas, notably in the cathedral cities, seaside towns and rural areas, and, thanks to the impact of the Chamberlains, in the West Midlands. The Conservatives had become the predominant English party after 1885 and their opponents were increasingly identified with the Celtic fringe. In 1906 this predominance had been shattered, but elections before and after resulted in a Unionist majority in the English constituencies.

	Conservative	Liberal
1885	213	238
1886	322	122
1892	261	190
1895	343	112
1900	332	121
1906	122	306
1910 Jan	233	188
1910 Dec	234	186

English Seats in the House of Commons

In local government the Unionists were well-established. After the creation in 1888 of the new system of elected county councils, political contests gradually crept in. Far from the outcome being beneficial to 'radical spendthrifts', as some Tories had feared, many of those elected were landlords who had previously served their area as magistrates. Counties adjacent to industrial areas returned more businessmen, but they also leaned to the Conservative side.

Unionists were active in other prominent positions in society. They heavily outnumbered the Liberals in the magistracy, to an extent that even some Conservatives found hard to defend. Magistrates were appointed only from men of wealth and substance. Before 1886 such men had been as likely to be Liberals as Conservatives, many of them still associating themselves with the forces of change rather than with those of resistance. But the crisis over the future of Ireland in the 1880s was a convenient opportunity for property-owners to switch over on a patriotic issue. Henceforth, the overwhelming weight of property was on the Conservative side.

The same was true in the world of commerce. In the City, the financial centre of London, the Conservatives were favoured by the 'money men' who liked their more cautious approach to public expenditure and their preference for lower taxation of the rich. The press also gave them strong support. The older provincial and pro-Liberal press of the 1850s and 1860s had been losing its popularity, and the new London-based 'nationals' were usually on the Conservative side. Liberal support in the newspaper columns ebbed away significantly after the Home Rule controversy of the 1880s.

In organisational terms the Conservatives were well-equipped and effective. Even if the machinery had been allowed to run-down in 1906, after years in which success had perhaps come too easily, by 1914 it was in better shape. The internal reforms shortly before the First World War had greatly improved efficiency. There was a network of Conservative Clubs and Associations, and the Primrose League had a mass membership of 800,000, including many women, even if it was by then more of a congenial political and social gathering than a serious political force. These were all signs of solid Conservative strength and, although the leadership of Andrew Bonar Law was unimpressive, the party did not lack effective spokesmen in the House of Commons.

3 The Composition of Conservatism

> **KEY ISSUE** How was the composition of the parliamentary Conservative party affected by the changing nature of society in the nineteenth century?

In the nineteenth century Conservatism had undergone a number of changes as it sought to adapt to alterations in electoral conditions. What sort of people were to be found within the Conservative Party in parliament and the country, and whose interests did they represent?

At the beginning of our period, the Party was overtly one of landed property. Within parliament the typical Tory MP was a member of the country gentry. By 1914 this was not so. From the time of Gladstone's leadership of the Liberal Party, but especially after 1885, many members of the middle classes went over to the Conservative side. In the 1885 election for the first time there were more MPs returned representative of industrial and commercial property than of landed property, and it was to be within the Conservative Party that the rise in numbers was most evident.

	Landed %	industrial/ commercial %	professional %
1868	46	31	9
1885	23	50	16
1900	20	52	18

Occupations of Conservative (and in 1900 Liberal Unionist) MPs

The majority of middle-class MPs were still Liberals and the 1906 House of Commons which they so dominated has been called 'the first middle-class parliament'. But there is no doubt that by the late-Victorian and Edwardian periods the composition of the Conservative Party had significantly altered. The backgrounds of the Unionist members elected in the second election of 1910, when both parties gained broadly equal representation, illustrated the nature of the change. The new parliament was solidly upper and middle class in origin, with business interests having become even more important. One hundred and ninety-six Unionists had been to public schools (90 to Eton), whilst only 23 had a purely secondary education. By occupation, the Unionists comprised:

Financial	124
Landowners	123
Barristers/solicitors	66
Transport Industries	48
Heavy Industries	43
Merchants	20
Coalowners	10
Textiles	5

(Some MPs are counted twice, where they had overlapping interests.)

This change in the type of representation was not confined to the House of Commons. Of the peerages created between 1886 and 1914, more were awarded to business than to landed Conservatives. As the longest-serving Conservative Prime Minister in that period, it was the

Marquess of Salisbury, himself the supreme example of the traditional governing classes, who nominated many of the new creations to the Upper House. It would, of course, be wrong to draw too sharp a distinction between the Conservatives of landed backgrounds and those with a middle-class one, for many of the landowners in both Houses were owners of industrial concerns or had substantial shareholdings in them.

Nonetheless, the Unionist Party at Westminster, with its strong industrial and business element, was a very different body from the old Tory party of Lord Liverpool, and the change in composition was not without its tensions. Whereas in the 1840s the conflict between old Toryism and new Conservatism had been difficult to reconcile within the same party, the party before 1914 represented a broad spread of landed and other property. Yet there was still some ill-feeling, for members of the old ruling class felt that their traditional values and approach were under challenge. Lord Hugh Cecil, the son of Lord Salisbury, particularly despised Joseph Chamberlain as a man who had made his fortune in industry, and disapproved of much that he represented. The Cecil family disliked his whole approach to politics, and he remarked that: 'It appears to be utterly sordid and materialistic, not yet corrupt but on the high road to corruption'.

This change in composition to embrace the industrialist class was reflected in the Cabinet. In the nineteenth century Cabinets were well-stocked with country gentlemen, members of the landlord class. Some may have sprung from a commercial background but by the time they entered government they had bought themselves a seat in the country and had left their origins behind. Even the Disraeli Cabinet of 1874 had contained 10 aristocrats out of 17 members – and the rest were upper middle class. After this, Conservative Cabinets included more middle-class representation, albeit rather upper middle class. The Salisbury and Balfour Cabinets comprised a mixture of traditional aristocrats and lawyers and businessmen. They were a little less patrician, although the vast majority had been to public school and Oxbridge and were sufficiently wealthy that they did not need to work in paid employment. In the original Balfour cabinet of 21 members, in 1902, 9 were aristocrats, 10 came from the upper middle classes, 16 had been to a public school, (9 to Eton), 14 had been to a university, (13 to Oxbridge).

At the very top, leaders such as Salisbury and Balfour came from traditional ruling families. Both were men of high social standing and wealth who had long been involved in public life. However, the choice of Bonar Law in 1911 seemed to acknowledge the position of 'new wealth' within Conservatism. As an iron merchant, he symbolised the forces of business, and his type of background was to become more common over the next generation, with twentieth-century leaders such as Baldwin and Neville Chamberlain having a similar background.

At all levels in the party, from those near the leadership to those who held key positions in the party machine at Westminster and in the country, the old style of Conservative was still well-represented. But these men were supplemented by new men whose approach was different. They were a useful addition in that they provided the party with new funds.

The changing composition was not surprising, for at the end of the century the economic situation of the country was undergoing change. The landlord class had been seriously hit by the 'Great Depression' of the late-nineteenth century, for they had suffered acutely from the easy availability of cheap imported food from overseas. Prices of wheat and meat had dropped, and the amount of land given over to arable and dairy farming had declined. Many of the country gentry had seen their wealth reduced, and their significance in the national economy gradually declined. Britain had rapidly industrialised, and it was now industry and trade which were the most important forms of capital.

What had happened by the end of our period was that the forces of property of whatever type had gone over to the Conservative side. On the one hand, the Conservatives had gained the business element which had previously felt better-represented by the Liberals. Also, much of the landed element within the Liberal Party, mainly Whigs, had deserted and gone over to their rivals; Lord Hartington (the Duke of Devonshire) was one such example. Conservatism in 1914, therefore, included old and new wealth, and in its membership had become the party for many men of title and affluence.

4 A Party for the Working Classes?

> **KEY ISSUES** Among which elements of the working classes did the Conservative party gain most of its support? Why did a substantial number of working-class voters feel tempted to vote for a party more usually associated with the defence of property and privilege?

Conservatism in the nineteenth century was never restricted to the wealthy. Especially after 1867 this vote was too narrow to provide victory on its own, and needed reinforcement. It was important for the Conservatives to be successful in gaining some support from members of the lower-middle and working classes. In the redistribution of seats made for the 1885 election several new constituencies had been created in large towns and cities. Previously Conservative voters had been heavily outnumbered in those areas, for they were dominated by workers in the poorer central parts, but now they were able to gain representation. Lord Salisbury had noted that there was 'a great deal of villa Toryism which requires organisation', and certainly the Conservatives began to gain much support in the better-off suburbs.

Their efficient electoral machine enabled them to organise campaigns carefully, and particularly in London their 30 full-time party
agents (as against the Liberals' three) were effective in winning support among the labouring classes.

Much to the surprise of Lord Salisbury, the Conservatives regularly
obtained one third or more of working-class votes. By 1914 they
received considerable support from those who were swayed by deference, who felt that the Conservatives were the natural party of government and had the leaders 'born to rule'. For instance, they
performed impressively in rural areas where there was solid
Conservative leadership in the community from the country gentry,
on the Bench and in local government. They also did better where
class solidarity was less apparent. Where there was no strong middle-
class presence – Scotland, Wales and the north of England – they were
less successful, for these were predominantly areas where class antagonism could be significant. Where there was a solid middle-class
interest some workers were keen to identify with it, perhaps wishing
to upgrade themselves socially. Voting Conservative was a way of keeping up with the Joneses.

Lancashire was one working-class area where there was strong
Conservative support. Hostility to the Irish immigrants in the large
cities there was a factor, and the Liberals suffered from their identifi-
cation with this group. The Conservatives made a conscious and
untypical attempt to organise the industrial labourers of the North-
west, for the party leaders encouraged the formation of Conservative
Workingmen's Clubs alongside the more exclusively middle-class
Constitutionalist Associations. Disraeli had been wary of allowing separate organisations for working men.

In London the Conservatives similarly benefited from fears
aroused by immigration, in this case of the large number of Jews who
came to England in the late-nineteenth and early-twentieth century.
Party propaganda was effective in painting a picture of the
Conservatives as the party of English nationalism, of Monarchy, of
Empire and of Protestantism. It combined these elements together to
create an image of patriotism, and in the Boer War had the ideal
opportunity to appeal for re-election, 'not as Conservatives, not as
politicians, but as Englishmen'.

The Conservative working-class vote was, then, often deferential
and/or patriotic. It was also based on economic self-interest, for some
artisans considered that the party had a better understanding of their
needs. Skilled working men, who had been employed for the same
company for many years, might be promoted to foremen, and were
pleased to think of themselves as having middle-class status and saw
voting Conservative as an indication of social respectability. Apart
from foremen and other overseers of those who actually did the
manual work, there was a growing number of office workers,
especially in London, who thought of themselves as being lower

middle class rather then workers. Such people, often separated into superior neighbourhoods of the large cities, wanted to keep the benefits they possessed, and tended to associate the Conservatives with a good standard of living and plenty of employment. They were also aware of the tradition of paternalistic Conservative social measures, such as slum clearance, worker's accident compensation and other factory protection.

The combination of middle, lower-middle and working-class support provided the Conservatives with a firm electoral base. It was because they gained support from all sections of the community that they could claim that as a party they transcended class divisions. They were truly a 'national' party, whereas the Liberals depended more on the votes of the masses in the towns and cities. Conservatives could claim to speak and act for the nation, and were able to portray themselves as the patriotic party which stood for the interests of the whole community.

5 Attitudes to the Role of the State

> **KEY ISSUES** How did Conservatives react to the gradual increase in state power within the nineteenth century? For what purposes did they regard state intervention as necessary or desirable?

There had always been an element of paternalism in Conservative thought. Throughout the nineteenth century, there were Tory thinkers, writers and politicians who accepted the need for state activity. In particular, Lord Shaftesbury, the philanthropist, who as Lord Ashley had been a committed social reformer in the House of Commons between 1822 and 1851, felt a deep sense of moral obligation to those less fortunate than himself. Disraeli and the Young England group wanted to see the palace made safe by keeping the cottage content. Such Tories accepted the inequality which existed in a hierarchical society, but they wished to temper its excesses by tackling the worst abuses.

Since Disraeli there has always been a strain in Conservative thinking which has felt a sense of social obligation for the least privileged. Usually its exponents have sought to combine traditional defence of established institutions with a popular programme of reform. By the late-nineteenth century the question of state intervention was becoming more important because within the Liberal Party people were beginning to wonder whether government should assume a larger role. In 1906 Liberals were still not committed to extensive social reform, but as Lloyd George and Winston Churchill became more influential the party began to promote measures which pioneered the welfare state. How should the Conservatives now feel about such reform? Could they accept the social challenge of these 'New

Liberals' and show that they also favoured state action, or should it be opposed?

Whereas Liberals worried about the social question primarily for reasons of conscience, some Conservatives were anxious for a different reason. Various surveys had pointed to the unfitness of the nation, particularly of its working population. This had implications for national defence, and some members of the party saw the need for an improvement in the people's health. They urged Balfour to make local authorities feed necessitous schoolchildren, institute medical tests, and offer some relief to the temporarily unemployed, which he did in 1905. On school meals and tests, he felt that he could be 'as sympathetic as he liked, but there would be no increase in rates'.

Salisbury and Balfour were not in favour of any policy of significant social improvement. Though moderately paternalistic, they nonetheless upheld the rights of property. They accepted a society in which people were unequal as entirely natural. Furthermore, they feared that social reform would threaten the liberty of the individual. Bonar Law showed no greater enthusiasm, believing that people who wanted social reform would not vote Conservative anyway.

Lord Hugh Cecil, himself an MP, explained the thinking of the Conservative establishment in his book *Conservatism*. He related the current situation to the writings of Burke, and warned against any policy which smacked of Jacobinism, and 'the levelling principles of the French Revolution'. He felt that it was 'plain that to take what one man has and to give it to another is unjust, even though the first man be rich and the second man poor'. But could Conservatives support measures designed to help disadvantaged sections of the community, such as the poor, without this infringing on the rights of the rich? He recognised no entitlement on the part of the least well off to receive any help, but accepted that there could well be reasons for the state helping them. Charity, gratitude for services rendered and expediency might be such motives, and Conservatism could encompass all three of them. Cecil was willing to justify state help, but had no wish to see it develop along socialist lines for socialism involved 'the end of private property, the fall of traditional institutions, the collapse of Christianity, and the disruption of morality and family life'.

Reform which did not threaten established institutions and rights of property, and was relatively cheap, could have a place in Conservative thinking. Indeed, it might be right and prudent to go along with it. However, the scope of such change was likely to be rather limited. When it came to responding to specific measures, Lord Hugh Cecil and his Conservative colleagues in the House could agree that the proposals should be viewed on their individual merits.

Joseph Chamberlain had met with little Conservative support when he put forward a scheme for old-age pensions at the end of the nineteenth century, but he never gave up the idea. However, his increasing preoccupation with South African questions meant that the issue was no longer high on his list of priorities. In any case, the cost of the Boer War made any action very unlikely. Balfour felt able to say that 'Joe's war had stopped Joe's pensions'. Although the party leadership acted tactically and tried to make the Liberal attempt of 1908 to introduce old-age pensions unworkable by widening its costs, for thinkers such as Cecil the issue was the more traditional one. Pensions might 'weaken the fibre of the people', and therefore might seriously undermine the capacity to resist aggression in any future war.

6 The Conservative Approach

> **KEY ISSUES** To what extent was the nineteenth century Conservative party one of resistance to change? Under what circumstances might change be justified?

When reviewing their history, Conservatives like to see themselves as a party committed to peaceful change. They pride themselves on their patriotism and support for great institutions, and they like to point to the tradition of Tory Democracy, that legacy of Disraeli which still inspires many Conservatives today. These have been continuous themes in Conservative literature.

For a Conservative reviewing the situation in 1900, it was a matter of pride that the constitution had been preserved. The House of Lords still retained significant powers and had the ability to block measures which were considered too dangerous or too radical. The Church of England was still the established church in England, Scotland and Wales, the Union with Ireland was still in place, and the monarchy was secure. Of course, there had been necessary adaptations, of which Conservatives had sometimes been the instigators, as in 1867 over parliamentary reform, but there had been no revolutionary change.

In 1914 the situation looked less certain. The House of Lords had lost its permanent veto over legislation, the Welsh Church had been disestablished and Home Rule for Ireland was on the statute book, even if it was suspended for the duration of the war. Moreover, in the process, the country had undergone a constitutional crisis over the rights of the Second Chamber and Ireland had been taken to the brink of civil war over Home Rule. On both these issues, the Conservatives had acted in a way which jeopardised their claim to be the party of law and order.

In defending the constitution, Conservatives have wished to look after the interests of those who are protected by it. This involves many of the forces of rank and property who looked to Conservatism as a guarantor of their position. Yet if resistance to change and defence of self-interest have been an element in the party's history, it has always shown some shrewdness in knowing when to give way. The traditional element within Conservatism sometimes found it difficult to compromise, but usually some of its more far-sighted leaders have recognised the importance of broadening the electoral appeal and social base of the cause they represent.

Writers such as Coleman[1] have stressed the conservatism of Conservatism, seeing it more as reaction tempered by an instinct for self-preservation. Speaking of the party in 1900, he depicted it as 'still a party of resistance and survival, of obstruction and delay and, when necessary, of compromise in order to avoid worse'. More obviously sympathetic writers such as Lord Hugh Cecil, have also felt that change has too often come at the last moment. In *Conservatism,* he reviewed four great events of the nineteenth century which in his view were disastrous for the party. On the first three, Roman Catholic emancipation, the Reform Bill of 1832 and the repeal of the Corn Laws, he found his predecessors guilty of failing to promote gradual change when it was still possible. The timing of change was all-important, and for him on these occasions action was taken too late; on the fourth issue, the 1867 Reform Act, he felt that the measure was passed with too much haste!

There were times when the mood of MPs was to resist the tide of political and social progress, times when self-interest was placed before the interests of the whole community. Fortunately for the party, on both occasions a Peel or a Disraeli was on hand to reorganise the party, refashion its image and provide it with a broader appeal. Their characters and styles were very different, but each was seeking to help the party to adjust to changing conditions, and to commit it to a course of moderate reform. More sophisticated Tories could see the need to recognise the rights of Catholics in 1829, to accept the Reform Bill as 'a final and irrevocable settlement' in 1832, or to abandon agricultural protection in the early 1850s. Sometimes, realism came at the eleventh hour, but nonetheless it came. Adaptation was and has remained a part of Conservative history.

7 Old Toryism and Modern Conservatism

> **KEY ISSUE** How and why did the Conservative party become a party representing owners of all types of property within the community, rather than just landed property?

The party is a coalition which does not represent a single class nor a single, galvanising political idea. There was a time when it was to a large extent the political expression of the landed interest, but that was the exception to the rule. The party of Lord Liverpool does not bear a clear resemblance to the party of the twentieth century, for he was the product of an essentially pre-industrial rural society. However, the party of Peel does, for he seemed to represent the new industrial society.

Peel was the first recognisably modern leader, the one who converted Toryism to a policy of moderate, cautious reform. The landed interest was preoccupied with the Church, the position of the monarchy and the protection of private property. They knew little and cared less about industry. Peel's ministry was concerned with the problems of the Industrial Revolution, and the movement to free trade. Old Toryism was rooted in the feudal tradition, hierarchical, authoritarian and paternalistic. Conservatism was to take that aristocratic and Anglican tradition from the past, and to graft on to it the aspirations of the middle classes. The Conservatives were to become, from Peel's day onwards, the party representing an alliance of the different forms of property – landed, industrial and commercial. By 1914, they were the safe haven for owners of all types of capital, what one writer has called 'a party of property and patriotism'.

Peel's contribution to the development of Conservatism in the nineteenth century was to refashion the party in such a way as to bring its thinking up to date, and to provide a model of constructive opposition and sound, competent administration. He ensured that the party was national in its appeal, and not the preserve of only the landed interest. Disraeli also strongly believed in the need for the United Kingdom to be one nation, and the Tory Party to be national in its embrace. He did something else. As Ian Gilmour,[2] one of the now-diminishing brand of 'wet' Conservatives, has discerned, he was 'able to bring warmth to Conservatism, and to add to its basic common sense a degree of romance, generosity and excitement, which . . . many Conservatives . . . are usually unable to express'. Of the 'basic common sense', there is room for debate. But of all Conservative leaders from the early-nineteenth century up to the outbreak of war in 1914, it was Disraeli who has been the greatest inspiration of the modern party.

Inspired leadership is a quality that all parties need from time to time. Some leaders have the good fortune to take over the reins at a propitious time, when their party is riding high in popular opinion. Others, capable in their own way, are less lucky for someone has to lead when the party is in a period of prolonged opposition, something to which the Conservatives have not been accustomed for much of the nineteenth and twentieth centuries, although following the 1997 election defeat their prospects for some years ahead seem bleak.

Parallels can be misleading, but what is often called the 'crisis' of the Edwardian Conservative Party has its echo today. In 1906, 1997 and 2001 the Conservative Party suffered huge defeats, its MPs reduced to 157, 165 and 166 respectively. After each setback, opposition in the new Parliament proved to be a dispiriting and uncomfortable experience, for Conservatives faced what was in effect a broad swathe of members of progressive leanings which made it unlikely that they could make a significant impact on events. In such circumstances, there was much internal contemplation, as right-wing MPs talked increasingly to those who were committed to the cause, rather than to the wider electorate. As they turned in on themselves, they seemed to lose sight of the need to appeal to a broad mass of voters and instead embroiled themselves in internal dispute, especially over tariff reform in Edwardian England, over Europe and other issues today. The leader, be it Balfour, John Major, William Hague or Iain Duncan Smith was in the unenviable position of trying to achieve unity and agreement between members of divergent outlook, many of whom did not really want to see any accommodation.

Through all its past difficulties, the Conservative Party has had a remarkable ability to survive and flourish. The resolution of the tariff issue was painful and difficult to achieve, but the party did stage a revival in 1910 and as Britain approached the outbreak of war the party acquired a sharper, if controversial, focus. By contrast, the defeat of 1997 was followed by an almost equally dire result four years later and the 'crisis of Conservatism' remains unresolved.

The past record of the Conservatives suggests that their ability to transform themselves and update their image, organisation and policies to meet the needs of the day stands them in good stead. As Conservatives agonise over the type of party to which they wish to belong and what their party should stand for, the outlook would appear to be discouraging this time around. Yet although other parties come and go, it is likely that in some form the Conservative Party will long continue, for the 'forces of conservatism' are an enduring element on the political scene.

References

1   B. Coleman, *Conservatism and the Conservative Party in Nineteenth Century Britain* (Arnold, 1988)
2   I. Gilmour, *The Body Politic* (Hutchinson, 1971)

Further Reading

Historians and the Conservative Party

There has been little by way of a continuous study of the character, personalities, policies and organisation of the Conservative Party – certainly not at a level which is meaningful to the student at 'A' Level or in the first year in Higher Education.

Two surveys provide a more-or-less continuous history. **R. Blake**'s *The Conservative Party from Peel to Thatcher* does not purport to be a comprehensive analysis of the party's history, but nonetheless is a fascinating book to read, not least because of the parallels it draws with more recent political circumstances. **J. Ramsden**'s *An Appetite for Power: A History of the Conservative Party since 1830* has several relevant and useful chapters. **S. Ball**'s *The Conservative Party and British Politics, 1902–1951*, **B. Evans** and **A. Taylor**'s *From Salisbury to Major: Continuity and Change in Conservative Politics* and **A. Seldon** and **S. Ball**'s *Conservative Century: the Conservative Party since 1900* are excellent reviews of the late nineteenth and twentieth centuries. **B. Coleman**'s *Conservatism and the Conservative Party in the Nineteenth Century* is a stimulating read, for his judgement is not clouded by any bonds of sentiment towards the party. He sees its raison d'être as being primarily to defend the self-interest of its members and to hold back social progress and change. Conservative thought is carefully analysed by **F. O'Gorman** in *British Conservatism*, a survey which covers thinkers from Burke to Thatcher.

Two short, but stimulating, works are **F. O'Gorman**'s *The Emergence of the British Two-Party System, 1760–1832* and **E. Evans**' *Political Parties in Britain, 1783–1867*, which differ on their view of the extent of party activity in the early period. Also on the first half or so of the nineteenth century, **R. Stewart**'s *The Foundation of the Conservative Party 1830–1867* is an illuminating guide. The same author has written more generally on *Party and Politics 1830–1852*. The Edwardian period is well-surveyed in **David Dutton**'s *His Majesty's Loyal Opposition: the Unionist Party in Opposition 1905–1915*.

Several biographies and specialised works are invaluable, though some are more suitable for teachers. In particular, **Gash** on Peel, **Blake** on Disraeli and **Robert Rhodes James** on Lord Randolph Churchill, throw an illuminating light not only on the persons of whom they write but also on the attitudes and policies of other personalities of the day. The works of **Paul Smith** and **E.J. Feuchtwanger** on Disraelian Conservatism offer interesting and penetrating analyses of their chosen areas. More recently, much has been written about the Salisbury era. **P. Marsh**'s *The Discipline of Popular Government: Lord Salisbury's Domestic Statecraft 1881–1902* is a comprehensive but for our purposes over-lengthy survey. The same is perhaps true of two recent biographies, those by **A. Roberts** (*Salisbury: Victorian Titan*) and **E.D. Steele** (*Lord Salisbury: A Political Biography*).

Index